SAFELY PRODUCTIVE

Linking Psychology to a Safe and Productive Culture

VAWN JEDDRY

ISBN: 978-1-7167-6842-2 (sc)
ISBN: 978-1-7167-6841-5 (e)

Library of Congress Control Number: 2020913693

Lulu Publishing Services rev. date: 07/24/2020

Knowing yourself is the beginning of all wisdom.

—Aristotle

CONTENTS

FOREWORD

I am very excited about this book. But before I go there, I first have to let you know a little about the author, Vawn Jeddry, as that will likely help you understand where this book comes from and why it is here. Vawn is one of the most amazing people I have ever had the privilege of knowing. She is extremely intelligent, both intellectually, and emotionally. And Vawn Cares!

At JV Driver, one of our Core Values is to Take Care of Each Other. As construction workers, if we don't take care of each other, I am not sure who else will. In the 20 plus years I worked with Vawn, I loved watching her work, and seeing how much she cared for all the people in construction that she came in touch with.

As Vice President of Health and Safety at JV Driver, Vawn helped us build a world class safety system. We built a fantastic culture that is still alive and well throughout the company that stressed taking care of each other. It is not policies, procedures, or rules that keep people safe, it is people, having a truly caring culture. At JV Driver, we have not had a lost time accident since 1994, on tens of millions of manhours of work. Our Total Recordable Injury Rate annually runs between 0 – 0.25 based on 200,000 hours. Our three year running average TRIR is below 0.15. Vawn and her team developed the core system around this, and she was also very responsible for helping build the right culture of safety, and productivity.

However, no matter how good the systems and culture were, Vawn agonized over every incident, whether a recordable (some call these medical aids), a first aid, or a near miss. What else could we be doing that would get us to zero's across the board. After parting with the company during one of the toughest resource capital spending recessions ever, Vawn took the time to look at "What Next", and this is where this book comes from.

What next is about helping construction workers to truly understand themselves, and what makes them tick. Why they react certain ways to certain circumstances. Why they have trouble leading is some cases, or dealing with people in other cases. Her thesis is, if we can help the workers understand themselves better (and it is a fair bet, that most construction workers have not spent much time understanding phycology, and specifically their own physiological make-up), and understand their crew better, we can help move the needle to zero's with this step. Why do I do what I do, and why does he do what he does? Crews, and their supervisors, understanding the behaviors of each other a little more clearly, and how to get the best out of each other, will help get us there. Having the policies, procedures, rules, and overall system while capturing the Hearts and Minds of the workforce and facilitating their understanding of their personality type and that of others, should move us that last step.

This book is for the individual crew member. Vawn can also deliver this training to your crews, which I would encourage all construction companies to take, if you would like to see a major improvement in keeping your teams safe. I have also encouraged Vawn to do 2 future books tying this into supervisor safety and productivity leadership training, as well as a company culture and systems training. I hope she gets the opportunity to follow through on these, as she could help so many marginal performing companies improve substantially, and in the process reduce harm and save lives of the construction workers she loves so much.

Take time to read and understand this book. Let it speak to you. I know most of the individuals she writes about here. I have seen the transformation of many workers go from Safety is an expense or a hassle to a way of life, and when they do, they plan the work, work the plan, get far better productivity, and keep people safe. You can make that transformation as well. Vawn is supplying a major tool for you in your toolbox for keeping people safe. I highly recommend you learn from it and you use it in your daily work and home life. It will help you become a better you, a better husband, wife, son, daughter, worker, foreman, leader and team mate. You will get out of this what you put into it. I hope it is a lot.

Take care and stay safe.
William (Bill) Elkington

Bill Elkington is the Chairman of a large multi enterprise construction business operating across North America and the UK.

PREFACE

As I look at my work boots, I feel a little sentimental. I can't help but think about all the things they've seen and heard while they've carried me around from site to site, region to region, and country to country.

My boots carried me when things were good—and when they were not so good. I remember putting them on at 4:00 a.m., and taking them off at 10:00 p.m. My boots and I have a long and complicated history of learning, teaching, screwing up, fixing, starting new things, and closing the door on others.

I'm by no means unique. Every morning, safety meetings in the construction industry are full of people with the same long, complicated relationships with their boots.

When you start a new job, it's exciting. Equipment, people, and materials come into the site, and trailers begin setting up as you try to look like you are making progress when you can't even find a plug to make coffee. Excavations start up, rebar and concrete arrive, and cranes go up. You also notice there is a little less elbow room at the lunch table.

From the project helm, you hear that consistent and familiar message that you hear in every job: "Work safely."

Throughout the project, you hear lots of other things too: "Be productive! That's too expensive. Why is it taking so long? What's the holdup?" And if you listen carefully, you will notice that these things are always bookended with the same message again: "Work safely."

Each workday starts with coffee, mixed with a little cynicism that the same old problems will persist and a little optimism that they won't. You are determined to find a way to be safe and productive. Sounds easy enough, right? Well, put on your boots and follow me because those lunchrooms are full of folks who struggle to find the sweet spot between safety and productivity. Throughout their jobs, they work to strike that balance.

You hardly notice the thing that you were there to build, and before you know it, it's all over and it's time to say goodbye to the people who have become dear friends and extended family members. You take your boots, look for the next job, and hope you will see them all again soon.

You'll remember the ones who couldn't find a way to be both safe and productive. Sometimes they stayed, and sometimes they didn't. Many times, finding the balance didn't happen, and they found themselves in the middle of a serious incident or infraction. Before they knew it, they were off to find their next job, feeling perplexed and believing they were doing what was asked of them.

The ones that found the balance remained: steady, sure, and confident. For these unicorns, the work is the work, and there isn't a safe or an unsafe way to do the job. It's just the work itself, done safely and productively with quality, pride, and vigilance.

It's for all these workers—friends and extended family members— that we write and share what we know about in this book. If you're reading this, it means that you bring unique gifts and talents to the world. You see things differently, and you make decisions based on a different set of learnings, experiences, and environments. You are one of a kind and irreplaceable, and a *safely productive* mind-set applied to your talents will make every work site that you and your boots visit better because you were there. By knowing yourself, you will find valuable insights that will fascinate you and give you the tools to help you lead a healthier and more fulfilled life.

This book, and the things I've learned from decades of working in the construction industry, is my humble contribution to the great people in construction. I hope that learning about human psychology, behavior, paradigms, and how they influence decisions and actions will shed light on your path and help bring you the clarity to yourself and those who rely on you to be *safely productive.*

INTRODUCTION

How many times have we heard that it's all about the people—people working together, sharing a common vision of what success looks like, and believing what is possible? "It's all about people," they say, and I believe them, which is why I wanted to write this book.

All my life, I have been lucky enough to be surrounded by good, hardworking people whom I admired very much. I have worked in trucking, mining, oil and gas, forestry, and power generation for most of my adult life, and what has made it a spectacular journey of learning has been the people I was blessed to work with. I have wonderful memories of smiles, laughs, love, sharing hard times, making friends, and feeling a sense of family. There isn't a job that I don't look back on and feel gratitude that I got to work with those wonderful people.

For the past twenty-five years, I have worked alongside the folks who made this industry great. The payroll people worked against hard deadlines to make sure everyone received fair pay for their work, and the procurement people scrambled to gather the material and equipment. They sometimes had to contend with delays and unhappy superintendents, but they kept going, working to do the very best job they could.

The superintendents and general foremen were looked at in awe by many of the folks on the team, but most of them never understood why. They didn't often see how commanding their presence was; after all, they were just being themselves.

Each trade has its own personality. A good friend of mine once told me that millwrights were like Vulcans: very logical and methodical in their thinking. The scaffolders were always bringing a solution, whether you needed a scaffold built around an eighty-foot tower or a set of seats in the smoke pit. The ironworkers often ran the show until the pipefitters came in and outnumbered them. You couldn't help but be proud when you saw a structural crew hoisting steel or setting in a large vessel. They worked in tandem with the cranes, and seeing them in action was a sight to behold. The heavy equipment operators made the machines an extension of themselves; I could watch them for hours.

The frontline supervisors were often the unsung heroes of the site. They arrived early, planned their day, walked the site, and attended the meetings to motivate the crew toward safe productivity. They often didn't get many breaks as there was an ever-flowing deluge of questions on payroll, meetings, work plans, safety, productivity, and scheduling issues. They often didn't get to have their sandwiches in peace, but they never stopped being the frontline leaders, and they always took the time to try to help.

I could go on and on about the people I have encountered and why I admire and see the beauty of the industry so dearly. The long and short of it is that my years in safety have been a blessing. To actually have been able to work every day with family and friends to help create a safe place to be was one of the greatest gifts I ever received, and I will always be grateful and humbled.

It's time to look at the people of construction and how we take care of each other. To do this, we need to look at ourselves as individuals first— as human beings—and understand our psychology and what makes us tick. It's time we learn about who we are and use the abundance of tools out there to understand ourselves and what motivates us to take risks and work safely and productively.

People also say that safety is personal because it is. We will all do all sorts of things for our own reasons. It is not because someone told us that we had to; it's within us to be the best versions of ourselves. However, we need the tools, knowledge, and skills to find that balance.

We know that statistics matter when winning project awards, but we don't always think about how for every injury statistic, there is a human being behind that number with hopes, dreams, aspirations, challenges, sorrows, and successes. They have families, friends, pets, and people who care about them and love them immensely. They are people with their own experiences and personalities that make them who they are. These folks, and the people on their teams, drive the industry and bring concepts to life. They are not just an industry; they are an industry full of wonderful individuals who make this world richer.

Let's talk a little bit more about statistics. I have worked with the good people at the Construction Industry Institute (CII) from the University of Texas at Austin. They have made it their mission to bring powerful tools and processes to the construction industry to enable us all to be safer, more productive, and cutting-edge in terms of technology and learning.

By working with their membership each year, CII collects injury and safety-related data from hundreds of projects. In 2017, their studied work totaled 2.9 billion hours worked in construction.

The following CII chart shows how safety performance has improved and how the decline of recordable injuries has reduced overall. As you will see, a consistent theme over many years is what we, as an industry, can't break to reach zero recordable injuries.

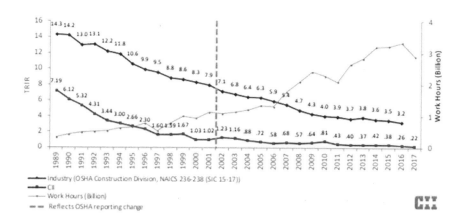

The story here is that the CII members report an annual total recordable injury rate of and nonmembers working in the general construction industry in the United States still report .22, which translates into "best-in-class performance." I believe that the work CII does has had a significant impact and has helped us make great strides in providing safer workplaces.

The general construction industry reports an average recordable injury rate of 3.2 as of 2016. That means that for every 2.9 billion hours of construction work performed, 4,600 people are injured to the point that they have required a physician's care, have suffered lost time, or have been fatally injured. Those 4,600 people have ended up with broken bones, severe lacerations, head injuries, back injuries, or exposure to chemicals or biological hazards. They are 4,600 individuals with families, friends, pets, and people who love them.

These numbers don't include all the near-miss events, damages, and first aids. They don't include the cases where someone is almost crushed by a piece of mobile equipment. They don't include the cases where a million-dollar piece of equipment is dropped from the forks of a forklift, and they don't count every time a worker has to leave the site to visit First Aid for a multitude of injuries or many other types of occupational illnesses. Those 4,600 individuals get hurt working to pay their bills, feed their families, take a holiday, and just live their lives.

Don't get me wrong. I'm happy for the advancements made since 1989. We have seen a decline in recordable injuries, and I'm grateful for the work and energy put in by all team players to get us moving in the right direction. We just can't seem to get to *zero loss*, which simply means no loss of people, equipment, environment, or reputation as a result of an incident.

Companies and owners have struggled to understand how we, as an industry, achieve *zero loss* and prevent these thousands of injuries. Many believe that policies, processes, and lots of paperwork have gotten us this far, but policies can only get us so far. Now it's about us, our hearts, and our minds. I'm talking about the hearts and minds of every person working on the projects, including the owners, engineers, contractors, and workers. We are all individuals with our own distinct worldviews and personality traits, and we are all on different legs of our own journeys through life. Our psychology plays a role in our decision-making. So I submit that what will get us to *zero loss* and strong productivity is *the individual.*

In this book, I want to talk to you about *you.* I want to talk to you about your paradigms and worldviews around our industry, your individual psychology, and how you view safety and productivity. For the purpose of our book, I want to have a good discussion about your paradigms around safe productivity. Do you see this as completely attainable—or do you believe you can only have one or the other?

I have always believed that a productive crew is a safe and happy crew. I firmly believe that we need to be excellent at both—being highly productive, capable workers and having a strong lifelong commitment to taking care of ourselves, our minds, and our bodies.

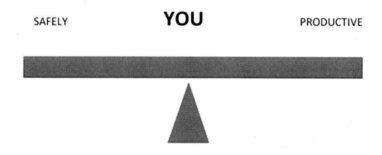

SAFELY   **YOU**   PRODUCTIVE

Aristotle said, "Knowing yourself is the beginning of all wisdom," and that's precisely what this book is about.

This is an opportunity for us to start a long-term dialogue on becoming a stronger industry by building a healthier and more fulfilled workforce. I believe this is our opportunity to look at ourselves as individuals and at how our healthy bodies and minds can contribute to the team, the organization, and the industry on a much deeper level.

Now, it's time for you to learn who you are, why you make the decisions you do, and why you feel the way you do in certain times of your life. Don't you think we have all spent enough time trying to figure out other people? Let's set that aside and put those efforts toward understanding ourselves first so we can become the best we can be.

When we are at our best, we are balanced, wise, and willing to give ourselves, our knowledge, and our time to others while taking care of our physical vessel.

CHAPTER 1
HOW THIS ALL WORKS

This book is written for you, the construction worker, and it doesn't matter if you're an engineer on a large project, framing houses, building scaffold, installing swimming pools, or building a refinery; this is for you.

We all try to maintain a balance between being productive and staying safe so we can continue to provide for ourselves and those we love. Some of us have worked on large projects where buckets of money were spent on promoting a safe work culture. Sometimes it tips to the point of little productivity because of the many steps, permits, and processes required to ensure zero harm.

On the other hand, some of us work for employers that are concerned with productivity at all costs. The trouble is that the cost is usually to you. In this productivity-dominated culture, very few resources are spent on ensuring zero harm to the workforce, and we find ourselves having to rely only on ourselves to make safe decisions. Sometimes we find a buddy to watch our back, and we watch theirs.

This book is intended to be a manual of sorts when it comes to finding a balance between these two critical elements of construction. So let's look at our two priorities and dig a little deeper.

- Who wants safety?
- Who wants productivity?

Who Wants Safety?

You

You don't want to get hurt, get into an accident where someone else is hurt, damage equipment that could result in job loss, or lose any earnings or security.

Your Team

We all spend so much time together that our teams can often become our extended families. The camaraderie and the reliance we have on each other is humbling, and we want the best for everyone. I have been at funerals for team members we have lost due to lifestyle choices or mental illness. I have seen the shock wear off and grief set in. Seeing strong people with broken hearts was almost too much to bear.

The Employer

Employers don't want incidents and loss events to cause additional costs to the project. They need to control all project costs to help estimate future projects, and they want to prevent any increases in insurance premiums. Most importantly, they don't want to lose you from their crew because they have already made a considerable investment in you. Replacing you is not cheap.

They also want to be known as an employer that takes care of their people. This helps them build loyalty and a good reputation among the transient workforce they rely on. Employers use their strong performance to win more work, which is viewed as a win for the company and a win for the workforce and their families.

The Client

Many sophisticated clients carefully protect and nurture their public persona and reputations. Many of these clients operate globally, and any serious incidents will be reported and spread around worldwide. This can have a devastating impact on their business and the people employed directly by them. Larger publicly traded organizations provide considerable resources to ensure that safety remains a high priority on their projects, and they take loss events seriously and devote a lot of time, people, and financial resources to understanding why construction workers take risks and how to minimize them.

The Public

Many of us have come across a traffic accident, and we have experienced the delays that it invariably causes. When I talk about the public as it relates to safety on the jobsite, I consider the family members and friends of every worker to be members of the public with a keen interest in seeing their friend's families and community members stay safe while on the job.

Many of us have been impacted by a worksite incident where someone we cared about was affected, and the family also suffered the terrible consequences of a preventable worksite accident. Most of us know that when an incident occurs and workers are harmed, the public turns on the employer very quickly. They side with the individuals who go to work every day to put food on the table for those they love.

Who Wants Productivity?

You

We all want to go home at the end of the day feeling like we have accomplished something. It makes for a very long day when we are not busy, and it can seem like an eternity when we're waiting to be productive. It's frustrating when we have to stop a job because we didn't have something we needed like information, tools, or materials. It's also a real piss-off when we start a job, are then pulled onto something else, and then are pulled off again. Most of us like to start and finish a job because it gives us a sense of accomplishment and pride.

Your Team

Like you, your team is made up of individuals who care about their reputations and how they relate to the quality and quantity of work that they are able to deliver to their employer in a day. A productive crew that works well together, continuously strengthens their bonds, and works together to ensure the success of the entire team. There is a great deal of pride in a productive crew.

The Employer

A bid-based job is defined by the ability to get a project done on time and on budget. Productivity suffers when there is a lack of planning, when timely decisions aren't made, and when tools, materials, equipment, and, most importantly, labor aren't available. (This is not a complete list, but you get the picture.)

The Client

The client has made a considerable investment to have any project built and has gone through multiple tiers of approvals to ensure that adequate resources are provided for the project to move forward. The client has also made multiple commitments based on the crew's ability to remain productive and loss-free. Poor productivity results in detrimental impacts to the owner in terms of reputation and their ability to deliver a project within their estimate budget and commitments. Being able to protect the costs of a project effectively enables owners to continue to invest and grow their businesses.

The Public

We don't always consider public interest when we discuss productivity, but ultimately, the public's benefits are considerable when we consider the number of investments that come into a region if productivity rates are high and can be maintained.

Investments from large projects come with opportunities for any businesses that work with the project. The community benefits from higher employment. Everyone from retailers, suppliers, and subcontractors alike benefit when people are working. However, when a country, province, state, or region is reported to have lower than average productivity rates, the prospects of companies making investments in that region are significantly reduced.

As you can see, there are so many stakeholders involved in the construction industry when being both safe and productive. The stakeholders are as diverse as their reasons, and I hope to shed some light on the critical importance of safety and productivity in our industry by encouraging you to stay physically, emotionally, and mentally healthy so you are able to work to benefit your communities, home regions, and countries.

We all want safety and productivity for different reasons. The simple fact is that the work won't get done unless we are equipped with a strong plan and are engaged enough to see the project through.

So how does *psychology* relate to all of this? Well, it's the most significant and relevant part of this book because it has to do with *people*, which is one of the most complex and interesting parts of our industry.

We can have a site full of material, equipment, and tools, but the *people* decide if we are safe and productive.

The project expects and asks a lot of the workforce. I hear it all the time at scheduling and productivity meetings: the crew will do this, the team will do that, they will work weekends, nights, and overtime hours, we can change their shifts and break times, and so on. Often, nobody ever consults the employees. Decisions are made for them by managers that have likely never met them and certainly have no idea who they are as individuals. The project is highly dependent on the health and well-being of the workforce, but little time or effort is made to engage the individuals on the team.

Surprise! The crew is made up of individuals with unique goals, aspirations, dreams, challenges, sorrows, and things that they wait all year to do, and they have people who they can't wait to see every day. They have particular views of how the world works, which has developed over many years, influenced by many teachers, mentors, and guides.

They have distinct personality traits that they draw strength from or that they are battling with in the hopes of becoming a better human being or just surviving. They are individuals who have a set of experiences that have shaped how they work and how they view safety and self-preservation. They are people who can be motivated to accomplish wonderful things or left to linger without leadership and guidance, never fulfilling their highest aspirations.

They have stories that will break your heart or lift your spirit. They have experienced profound loss and can suffer from debilitating fear, anger, or shame, and depending on where they are in their journeys, they can be performing at their absolute best or barely be getting by.

This is the *crew*. They are individuals like you who have likely always been treated as part of a group and not the unique gift to the world that they are.

This book is about looking at all of these elements, including:

- You, your paradigms, and your worldview. How they came to be and how they impact your life.
- What safety on a jobsite means and how poor performance impacts you.
- Understanding the influence you have over your own productivity.

- Your distinct personality traits and levels of personal development. Each of us carries distinct traits that influence our behaviors and our paradigms. The levels of development are critically important as they measure how effective and healthy our minds are at any given time.
- Stories from the field, describing how construction workers have found a way to work safely and productively in their journey. They discuss how they moved from productivity-dominated cultures, and the challenges and opportunities they encountered along the way by using their strengths.
- Strategies on how to motivate and lead different personality types. Strong, balanced leaders tell us how the various traits can help motivate and lead individuals on the crew toward a *safely productive* mind-set.

Where does your life take you from here? Do you have a plan? You are a builder—so let's build your plan for the future!

We mentioned paradigms earlier, and in the next chapter, I would like to explore that a little deeper with you. We will look at how our paradigms are developed and how they impact us every day through our thoughts, behavior, and interactions and the results we get.

CHAPTER 2
PARADIGMS

"Hey, how are you?"

"Good, how are you?"

"Good, okay, catch you later."

Well, that was insightful. We really understand each other now.

Every day, we perform this ritual over and over. How many times has someone asked you how you are *really* doing? I bet you didn't have to use both hands to count. Ironically, how you are feeling, thinking, and believing is at the core of how safe you will be on the site today.

Ready for more irony? I bet you haven't actually taken the time to consider how you really are. Your programming tells you to say, "I'm good," but there is so much going on behind those safety glasses.

Let me tell you a little bit about my personal views (paradigms) around construction workers. They are the kindest, toughest, funniest, and most generous, caring, and talented people you will ever have the pleasure of working with. The work they do would stop you in your tracks. They do things that would make others woozy, but they have the skills, talent, experience, and drive to do the hard work; they do all the heavy lifting if you will, working long hours into the night.

Construction workers generally get up before everyone else, make their lunch, put on their boots, grab their coffee, and drive to the worksite. At lunch, they stand in line for the microwave, find empty coffeepots in the lunchroom (if coffee is supplied at all). They attend safety meetings, raise concerns that are sometimes addressed and sometimes not. They do their best to work safely and productively, and they try to do what is asked of them. They want to put in a good day's work for a good day's pay.

When they finish their shifts, they drive home when most people are already there, cleaning up their supper dishes. They get back late, feeling tired, and are probably frustrated by some silly thing that happened that was out of their control, where they were held accountable. They often fall asleep on the couch, shut off the television, and go to bed early because the sound of the alarm comes too soon. Then they do it all again tomorrow until the next project is built. They are realistic and believe they see the world as it actually is. And no one ever asks them how they really are.

Because I have these views and see construction people this way, it impacts how I behave. I have always strived to treat people on-site with dignity and respect, and I try to emulate the qualities of kindness, care, and compassion. When I achieve this, the results are everlasting friendships, collaborations, support, and focus on preventing any harm to these wonderful people.

Construction folks don't tend to talk about paradigms and feelings. It's not because they won't; it's because others rarely ask a construction worker how they feel and how they are. If they're not feeling good, then why don't they feel good? What's going on? Are they okay? Is there something going on?

The layperson's perceptions about construction folks are that they are rough and tough and curse a lot. Generally, that's true, but they are by and large gentle, wonderful, big-hearted people who can find the humor in most situations, and they would give the shirts off their backs to help a friend.

As someone who has chosen to work in this industry, you have likely lived a life where you were exposed to many sights, sounds, and smells (lunchroom smells could be their own chapter). You were raised with a set of beliefs, cultures, and values that were influenced by parents, grandparents, other family members, friends, teachers, and classmates. They all had a hand in building your worldview, your *paradigms,* and the lens through which you see the world.

By paradigms, I mean the perceptions, beliefs, and experiences that make up your paradigms. They provide a framework that you use to carry on with life and its daily demands. You use your experiences to help you navigate and interpret the various things you encounter.

You believe what you believe. You were raised that way. You grew up believing that the way you saw the world was the way it was. But is it? Have you examined your worldview lately? Have you cleaned the lenses that you see your life through?

Having our paradigms challenged is a hard thing to do because we love to be right. Our paradigms are what we know, they help us make sense of this world, and they keep us grounded.

To have your belief system challenged or even blown up completely can be a life-changing event. That's a scary prospect for someone who takes satisfaction in being right and being trusted by others. For many of us, it makes us feel happy and valued when we are seen as an authority or subject-matter expert. When you're used to being an authority, it's hard to step back and ask yourself if you really get something. *Is my paradigm distorted or just plain wrong? Is my lens cracked? Well, holy cow! Maybe it is!* And if it is, what can you do about it?

Your paradigms are complicated and have developed over a lifetime. For a minute, think about what your paradigms are around the people below. What is the first word that pops into your mind?

Work Groups in Construction	Your Paradigm (First Thought That Comes to Mind)
Engineers	
Politicians	

Pipefitters	
Ironworkers	
Project Managers	
Layoffs	
Safety Departments	

The first word that pops into your mind (good or bad) gives insight into your paradigms. Let's look at engineers. If you said they were great, and you believe they are always there to help (no one ever has by the way), that gives you a snapshot into your paradigm. If you said they hold up the work, then the next step is asking yourself honestly why you felt that way—and what experiences and conditioning led you to feel that way. You may find that your paradigms come from other people, from the industry, or from your culture. You may reflect on this and ask:

- Have I ever had a bad interaction with a member of the engineering group?
- What contributions do they make to help this thing get built?
- Do quick decisions on design changes ensure the safety of the people operating this thing we are building?
- Do we need them to keep the industry going?

If you are open to examining your paradigms and considering new information, you may find your paradigms need some tweaking. When further information becomes available, you may have your beliefs challenged and your views changed. This is a paradigm shift, and it almost always occurs when more information is made available and when you are open to considering that things could be different from what you believed.

A *paradigm shift* is a concept identified by Thomas Kuhn, an American physicist. When a paradigm shift happens, you experience a fundamental change in the basic concepts and practices you previously had. You see things differently, you feel differently, and you often behave differently. You will know that your paradigm has shifted when you stop judging and feel an urge to understand and help instead of criticizing.

If you have negative sentiments in any area of your life, take a look at your paradigms around the situation. Facts are friendly, and looking at a situation as it really is, through a clear lens, will help you stay focused on the things that truly matter.

I'm interested in learning about your paradigms concerning safety, the safety team, and the safety program. What is the first word that pops into your head when you hear these words? Are they good, bad, or indifferent?

Your paradigms around safety are foundational in finding the balance between working *safely* and *productively*. If the word *safety* makes you cringe, then that's a strong signal that your paradigm may need to be challenged if you are ever to find the balance. After all, if the goal is to find the balance, your core beliefs around safety must be examined carefully to understand why it causes these reactions.

If a part of you believes that you can't have safety and productivity at the same time, that one must suffer on the job, then what do you think you're going to do when you get to work? What are the behaviors that we would all see if we sat and watched you? For example, we might see:

- a project manager slashing orders for safety equipment and put cost ahead of comfort, form, and fit
- a design engineer choosing to rely on fall arrest harnesses and lanyards rather than finding engineered solutions to prevent falls from heights during construction
- a contractor owner choosing to pursue projects where safety isn't a high priority or not investing in safety
- a worker who does not use personal protective equipment, takes shortcuts, or uses equipment improperly

You are probably starting to see a pattern here. If somewhere in our belief systems, we still hold the worldview that safety is a cost, a pain, or something that slows production, then our behaviors will demonstrate that. We will do things that get us inferior results. In our case, it could be a serious event or even, God forbid, a fatality.

Imagine if you saw safety as a trusted guide and as a valuable toolbox of knowledge and information that would ensure your security and well-being. How would your behaviors change? How would that construction worker plan and execute their work? How would that engineer look at the design process? How would business owners choose to invest in safety?

Paradigm checks must be conducted by all members of the team, at all levels, and at all stages of project execution. As human beings, we all have a stake in keeping each other safe and free from harm.

A few years ago, I had a paradigm shift while investigating an incident at a pulp mill. A worker was seriously injured while loading a trailer. He was pinned between the load and one of the stanchion posts, resulting in a punctured lung. While I was working on the investigation, I was collecting statements and talking to the foreman in charge of the work. I got the feeling that he wasn't taking this seriously. He was downplaying the severity of the incident and was starting to irritate me. I asked if he had any idea how serious it could have been. He said, "More than you will ever know." He told me that he hadn't slept a wink since the incident happened. He was going over and over in his mind what he could have done differently. *Should he have talked to the worker? Should he have planned things differently? Should he have assigned another crew? What if he died? What would he tell his family? Should he quit now? Was he still fit to lead?*

The fact of the matter was that the incident was hitting him profoundly. It shook him at depths I had never considered. All I looked at was his behavior, and I had made up my mind that he didn't care. I couldn't have been more wrong.

At that moment, my paradigm changed. I wanted nothing more than to help him understand why it had happened and help get him— and the rest of the team—through the event. I wasn't mad anymore, and I felt tremendous compassion for what he was going through. I was ashamed, and it changed how I saw leaders and coworkers following an incident where a member of the team has been hurt.

I can't emphasize enough how important it is to be completely honest with yourself. Your paradigms are not bad or ugly. They are a part of who you are, and they have served and protected you over the years. They have helped you make sense of a changing and complicated world. They can sometimes just be ineffective and stop you from achieving all that you want in life.

Like you and your boots, you have a long, complicated history with your paradigms, and they have been with you through good times and bad. Every operator manual will tell you that regular routine maintenance will keep the equipment functioning and reliable. You and your paradigms are exactly the same.

You are a deserving, valuable, special, and talented asset to the world, and you need care and maintenance to function optimally. All positive, life-changing things begin with examining and cleaning our lenses and fixing the cracks. Examine your paradigms around safety. Do you simply comply because you'll get in trouble if you don't? Do you see it as a valuable friend who is along with you on your journey—and that by valuing all it can bring you is priceless?

For goodness sake, have a look at your lenses and clean them because how you view safety will influence what you do each day. What you do in every moment will get you positive results if your paradigms are based on principles—the fundamental truths that serve as the foundation for your system of beliefs, behaviors, and values.

Next, we will look at safety and how it rolls up into our industry, the reasons that it plays such a critically important role in our lives and why it is so personal. After all, I could talk about safety all day long!

CHAPTER 3
SAFETY

What drives your decisions around safety and risk-taking? Do you know? Could it be a lack of understanding actual risks? Could it be rushing around and taking shortcuts, being a blind follower, or wanting to be liked or admired? Or maybe you simply just don't care?

A few years ago, I took a holiday and went to Hawaii. While I was there, someone in a very colorful shirt, shorts, and flip flops asked if I wanted to go out on a boat about thirty miles offshore, get out of the boat, and into a cage where sharks would be swimming around me. Excited about the offer, I said, "Yes, please!" If a supervisor on an average construction site gave me similar instructions, with similar risk conditions, I'm not sure they would have received the same response. So why did I hop on that boat to swim with sharks when it was my choice?

Having reflected on this for many years, I sincerely believe that it came down to personal choice. We make choices based on the value we place on ourselves as human beings and the things we hold dear, like our well-being and our peace of mind. Options give us freedom. Having the opportunity to do what we believe is right for us is liberating. When we don't have a choice, it feels like we're shackled.

Being safe doesn't mean that we live our lives in bubble wrap; it means we are smart about the types and amounts of risk we take on, and we make intelligent choices about how we safely execute our work. We make the best decisions when our minds are clear, when we are focused on our highest priorities, and when we are healthy-minded and unshackled.

In the following case studies, you're going to hear about how things used to be in our industry—and how they still are in some cases. Productivity came at all costs, and safety wasn't discussed or even considered. Lives were lost, sites were cleaned up, and everyone went back to work. As fatality rates continued to climb, a paradigm shift happened in the industry that worksite fatalities were at unacceptable levels, and something had to change.

Governments, labor groups, and business owners started to look at training, safety programs, and updated legislation to try to change the landscape. Things improved gradually, and total recordable incident rates and lost time injuries decreased. Risk assessments, behavioral-based programs, inspections, and audits became routine on many jobsites.

People understood the expectation of safety and were largely compliant because they didn't want to get in trouble. Some say that there was so much safety that nothing got done or that productivity rates suffered because of the complexity of programs and the time it took to execute them.

Over time, safety became pretty complicated with rules upon rules, policies and procedures, and hazard assessments. In some cases, there was so much happening that it caused paralysis. People didn't know what to do and didn't want to make any mistakes, so they did very little. The people in leadership roles made the best decisions they could, but they didn't always know the right answers either.

Ultimately, the goal of this book is to get us to use the best parts of ourselves to make the safest choices that will get us home each day. You and your mind are the biggest resources that any project team has. The project you have committed to and your team members rely on you to bring all of your skills, talents, experiences, and especially you're a game to the job every day. If you aren't mentally and physically prepared to do the work, your mind-set can put you at risk, so you must take the necessary steps to mitigate any hazards that this presents.

Think about any time you were assigned a job. The supervisor provided you with your task for the day, and it could be anything from erecting a scaffold to stripping forms. It didn't matter what the task was. Once the job was assigned to you, it was your job to press the pause button and consider all of the risks and precautions that needed to be in place before you did the work. While the pause button was pressed, you should have considered your mind-set, your readiness to do the work, all the safety tools and processes that were available, and which ones you would use.

When I look at safety, I see it as an opportunity to press the pause button between being assigned the work so it can be executed and done productively.

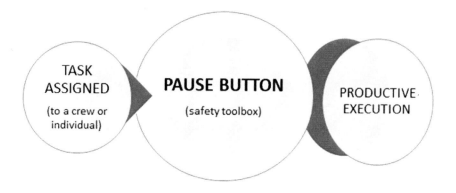

You can almost think about safety as another toolbox that you collect tools from before you go into the field. Once a task is assigned to a crewmember or an individual, you can press the pause button and consider all the things that could go wrong during the course of the work. The key things to consider while the pause button is pressed are as follows:

You

What mind-set are you in? Are you calm and focused? Do you understand the task and the steps required to do the job? Do you feel comfortable, secure, and equipped to do the work? If you are tired, distracted, or suffering from some type of anxiety or stress, this is a clear signal that your mind-set needs to be part of your risk assessment and how you will control the hazards that it presents.

Execution

Do you have a job plan? Do you fully understand the sequence of steps to productively execute the task? It is imperative that you understand what a successfully executed, *safely productive* job looks like. Consider these things:

- Are tasks with work steps clearly defined?
- Are risk assessments based on technical information?
- Do you understand the schedule and the time allotted to execute the task?
- Do you have access to all safety processes, procedures, and information that you need to complete productively?
- What if something happens?
- What's the worst thing that could happen? How will you handle it?
- What if there is an unexpected change?
- What if a tool malfunctions?
- Will you be ready to hit the pause button again and recheck your toolbox?

Toolbox Contents

The contents of the toolbox are limitless, and with the help of the safety team, leadership, and frontline supervisors, you should be able to access almost anything you need to work *safely* and *productively*. Contents can include at a minimum:

- the safety manual

- safe work procedures for high-hazard work
- safe work practices for tools and equipment used
- risk assessments (samples and to refer to when building new assessments)
- tool and equipment manufacturer's instructional manuals (everything for a safety harness to grinders)
- magazines/articles on safe execution
- self-assessments
- legislation

You should always take each opportunity to learn and to keep growing as an individual and as a team member. There are so many learning opportunities, both online and in the classroom, that you can take advantage of. We all have a responsibility to keep developing and honing our skills and knowledge. Imagine if a journeyman barber or stylist went to school thirty years ago and never took any type of follow-up training? We would all look like John Travolta in *Saturday Night Fever*. Instead, they stay up to date through continuing education and seizing new learning opportunities.

Once you fully understand the task in the sequence required to execute the job safely and productively, and you have considered and implemented all hazard controls needed to control any event or risk that could be present, you are ready to execute. Remember, other hazards that may need to be considered could be a distracted or an unfocused mind. Deal with distractions so that you are able to set them aside and execute the work with focus.

Implementing work mindfulness is so imperative to ensure that you are giving your full attention to the task that you are doing. A wise friend of mine told me that we need to be respectful of every task we do. What he meant by this was it doesn't matter if we are sweeping out the wash-car trailer or locking out a piece of equipment. The task deserves to be done to the highest standard. We must always do our best regardless—even if we do not like the task. By doing this, we respect the task.

By learning to treat our work in a ritualistic way, it will become a habit. We must put all of our efforts toward not letting our feelings guide us, and we must act on facts, information, schedules, and safety. As you execute your work to a high degree of safety by using all of the tools in your toolbox, you will find that you will become highly productive and stay safe at the same time.

So we have talked about some of the tools available to you in your journey to *working safely*. This is only the tip of the iceberg, but I hope you have a good understanding of how important it is to start each workday with a safety mind-set. The tools and resources available to you are vast and readily available if you have the desire to learn and continue to grow your expertise.

Just as important is the concept of *productivity*. We need both safety and productivity to ensure that our industry thrives. Our industry is more than capable of achieving both of these core competencies. In the next chapter, we will talk about what productivity means and the benefits and challenges to achieving this goal.

CHAPTER 4
PRODUCTIVITY

Think about yourself for a minute and notice how on some days it can be difficult to *feel* productive, let alone *be* productive. There are times when I can fill an entire day with tedious tasks that mean nothing and don't contribute to an overall goal. Most times, I can justify this because I was physically moving, even though I wasn't accomplishing a damn thing. I like being productive. I hate the feeling of not accomplishing anything of value. That is truly demoralizing for a lot of people, especially the people of construction who pride themselves on their ability to finish a project.

Dr. Stephen Covey said, "It doesn't matter how fast you're going if you're going in the wrong direction. Focus on the compass and not the clock." I always felt this meant that we could be racing through our lives, never heading in the direction that we were destined to go, and by the time our ninetieth birthdays come, we'd be disappointed with what we accomplished in life.

When I read Dr. Covey's writing now, I can apply this quote to almost anything, including working safely and productively. If we don't focus on safe and productive work, it doesn't matter how fast we complete a task if we place ourselves, the people we love, and our well-being at risk. On the other hand, if we work so safely that productivity and satisfaction for making progress is diminished, we simply will not feel a sense of accomplishment to the same extent we would if we worked safely and productively. Everyone talks about productivity, and it's almost always in a negative way. We often hear phrases like, "Productivity is low," "Productivity is poor," or "It's the workers' fault."

In fact, the rate of productivity—output produced by the hour worked—is largely tied to the decisions the leadership groups make. In saying that, I can't help but believe that we as workers have a responsibility to improve productivity. I believe that a big group of intelligent, skilled, motivated workers can transform the industry if they choose to do so.

I also hear that we now have so much safety that productivity has become a thing of the past. That's a paradigm closely held by a number of people in the construction industry. Some days, it feels this way for the people who are chasing permits and looking for information. They may be worried that they will do the wrong thing, so they carefully proceed, hoping they don't get in trouble for breaching a rule they likely didn't know about. Being *safely productive* is a mind-set based on the concept of working smarter, not harder, and the entire team putting their best efforts forward to keep productivity moving forward.

In my experience as a safety person, I have seen it over and over again—construction professionals who are productive are almost always more fulfilled, enjoy their work, and enjoy the learning that comes along with the job. They are also extremely safe because they understand the sequence of information that is available, and they have the correct tools and equipment. Most importantly, they are fully engaged, motivated, and accountable for their performance.

Earlier in this book, we talked about people and how they make all the difference to the success of a project. I think we agree on that, but we still need to recognize that there are some things that are outside of our control. Our job as construction professionals is not to spend time worrying about things we can't control and focus on the things we can control.

Many of the challenges can be managed if the superintendent/ management knows about them and has ample time to respond, but the significant productivity issues occur when the work is disrupted due to unforeseen problems where time to prepare alternate work plans is limited. The impacts of change can be significant.

Impacts of Change

When working at a steady pace and making good progress, disruption to our momentum can be frustrating and sometimes confusing. These changes consume field personnel hours and delay crews in continuing work in other areas. Frequent changes can quickly demoralize us, and our attitudes around change affect how we choose to respond.

When we complete a job and find that it has to be taken apart and redone, this can shake us up. We took pride in completing a task— only to find out there was a problem that should have been identified beforehand.

It's critical that construction documents are carefully examined to identify problems before the work is assigned to the teams. By doing so, we can reduce the psychological impacts that change has on motivation and attitudes. Keep the momentum going.

Weather Delays

Productivity can decrease substantially by extreme weather, which is often not adequately anticipated. It forces adjustments in schedules and work plans and possibly damages to completed work. When raingear, winter clothes, and other protective clothing must be worn, it can impede a worker's performance. Considerable attention should be paid to seasonal weather changes and their impacts on the crew. Alternate planning and realistic changes to the schedules factor in lower productivity during these times, which can alleviate pressure on the workforce and their leaders to make up the lost hours due to the inclement weather.

Material Problems

Late material deliveries often require crews to move to new areas and reinitiate work activities. Shortage of materials can also result in temporary crew layoffs. Leadership can alleviate pressure on the crew by carefully and meticulously examining construction documents to ensure that all required materials are on-site and prepared in advance. If at all possible, don't send the workers to the field unless they have the tools, materials, equipment, and information they need to complete their task.

HIGH LABOR TURNOVER

High labor turnover is an indication that multiple problems exist including:

- poor planning
- low morale
- lack of leadership

When we feel that we can no longer make a difference, or that things will not improve, we become demoralized, and productivity slows significantly. As a construction team, our challenges are to look for opportunities that are within our control to bring about positive change.

Multiple strategies can be used to support supervisors and workers to fully engage the workforce and move productivity in the right direction. Workforce training and development plans need to be consistent with the goals of the project. For example, if a large portion of the work involves confined space entry and working at heights, budgets should allow for this vital worker training.

By working together to identify the training needs, improvements in productivity will occur simply because the crew knows what is expected of them and how they will do it. These things can have a significant impact on morale and engage the team toward the project goals.

In my humble opinion and based on many years on-site, I've summarized a productivity table to describe some key elements that could have a positive impact on jobsite productivity. I'm not so arrogant as to say that I am an expert in worksite productivity, but I believe that this is a good starting point for us to think about how we can engage and do our part to improve the productivity problem.

Productivity		
People / Paradigms	Material/Equipment	Information
Engaged	Available	Sequence available
High morale/motivated	Assembled prior to crew assignment	Drawing available
Trained/capable	Correct/appropriate for job	Workforce open
Informed	Quantity correct	Schedule available and understood
Accountable	Complete based on drawings	Priorities understood

People and Paradigms

Firstly, the most important factor is to look at yourself. After all, all we can change is ourselves, right? Do you have all the ingredients you need to develop a productive mind-set? If you look at the table above under "People/Paradigms," we talk about being informed, accountable, engaged, trained, and capable. This should be your checkbox. Are you these things, and if you're not today, are you willing to do the things you need to get there? Here are some examples:

1. What, if anything, can you do to improve your training and knowledge about the work you do? Do you wait for somebody to bring you a training program or take the initiative? Are you accountable to continuing your own learning without somebody holding your hand?

2. Do you put too much confidence that if there's something you need to know, that somebody will tell you? Do you wait for someone to come and make sure that you're informed, aware, and understand the plan? Or do you make it your priority to seek out the knowledge you need to do the job safely and productively? How much accountability do you have to ensure that you were prepared for the work?

3. Are you engaged and motivated to see this project or task through to the end, and give each task in your job the respect it deserves? Are you looking at the clock or the compass? Are you headed in the right direction—or are you more concerned with how quickly you get there?

Productivity Paradigms

Like we talked about before, as people of construction, we also must take a hard look at our paradigms around productivity and what it means, including all the factors that create obstacles to becoming truly productive. We should all be on the lookout to improve ourselves when it's within our control to influence positive change.

In the next table, challenge your paradigms around the following issues. Think about what role you could play in improving these things:

Productivity Challenge	**Your Paradigm** **(First Thought That Comes to Mind)**
Lack of supervision or poorly trained supervision	
Leaders not making timely decisions	
Improperly trained craftspeople	
Incidents or other unplanned events	
Poor coordination of work activities	

Insufficient tools, materials, or equipment required to do the work	
Poor jobsite layout, location of parking, or tool cribs	
Absenteeism, high employee turnover, low morale, or worker attitudes	
Adverse weather, poor lighting, too cold or too hot	
Excessively moving workers from job to job	
Uncontrolled start or end times, uncontrolled breaks	
Poor use of multiple shifts	
Construction mistakes, rework due to missing, wrong, or incorrect drawings	
Changes to plans	

All of these things impact the hourly output per unit and can create a long day full of confusion and chaos. When productivity is affected, so is the worker, as most of us measure the success of our days by how much we get done. When we work in chaos and confusion, it's challenging to remain operating at our peak performance levels because we can become demoralized and disengaged.

It's normal to look at a list like this and blame the leadership entirely, but I would ask you to challenge that paradigm. Can we, as key, critical members of the project, hold no accountability for our part in less than stellar productivity? I don't think it's reasonable to say that it's solely one group's fault because if we are all in this as a group of high performing individuals, we are absolutely accountable as one team. Let's take a quick look at the issue around poorly trained supervisors. If each member of the crew took an active role in alleviating the pressures around supervisor training, could we influence positive change? If we decided to engage and take meaningful action together, we could make the projects better for all.

In the following diagram and table, we illustrate how everything starts with how you think and how you see the world around you. What you think and believe drives what you do and how you behave every day in life. Your behavior in life gets your results. If the results you get are not what you want or make you feel unbalanced—working productively while disregarding safety—you must have a good look at your paradigm and reevaluate whether it is aligned with the results you want.

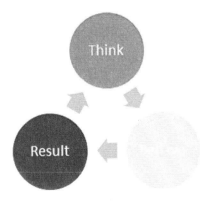

Think. What are your paradigms around supervisors and the training they receive? Are they healthy and helpful? Is it sufficient or should they be fully supported to develop their skills to effectively lead? Is there anything you can think of to support your supervisor using your skills and talents?

Behave. Is there anything that you can do to help, support, or alleviate that problem?
By improving your own skills and learning, could you help the problem?

Result. By developing your skills and abilities, would it help the supervisor to better plan the work and allocate the resources? Would it free them up to pursue learning of their own to become stronger leaders? Could it allow the supervisor additional time for planning and coordination?

We must recognize that how we feel impacts how we behave, and our behavior has an impact on our performance and the results we get. If we were to look at each productivity challenge separately, can all of us work together to alleviate the obstacles one at a time?

Productivity: Daily and Weekly Tools

President Dwight Eisenhower said, "What is important is seldom urgent, and what is urgent is seldom important." He developed a simple but effective tool for prioritizing our most important tasks. Along with reexamining our paradigms, we can also select the most important things we can do to reinvigorate productivity and work on the most important priorities, resulting in a more satisfying day.

The great thing about Eisenhower's matrix is that it can be used for broad productivity plans (*How should I spend my time each week?)* and for smaller, daily plans (*What should I do today?*). Stay in the green area (see the chart below), and your productivity will increase. You will have more time for the important things and feel more like you are in control of your own destiny.

Eisenhower's strategy for taking action and organizing tasks is simple. Using the decision matrix below, you will separate your actions based on four possibilities:

1. Do Now: Urgent and important (tasks you will do immediately).
2. Schedule: Important, but not urgent (tasks you will schedule to do later).
3. Delegate: Urgent, but not important (tasks you will delegate to someone else).
4. Delete: Neither urgent nor important (tasks that you will eliminate).

Eisenhower's Productivity Matrix

	Urgent	**Not Urgent**
Important	Do Now These are things that relate to staying productive and executing your schedule. It can be based on an urgent client request.	Schedule Schedule a time to do it. These are things like making time for personal development, learning, planning, preparation, and team building. It also includes family time and physical activity.
Not Important	Delegate Give it to someone else. These are based on other people's emergencies and pointless meetings. If they impact what you are doing, say *no* to these activities.	Delete Eliminate it. These are time wasters such as Instagram, Twitter, Facebook, complaining, smoking, and surfing the internet.

So you may be asking yourself, "Why would I do that? Why would I help them? It's not my job." Well, I'll tell you that people who function at their best strive to contribute to the health of the entire team without hesitation because they have found a way to bring the best version of themselves to the world. They focus on things like:

- being giving
- being humble
- collaboration
- generosity

- gratitude
- loyalty
- teamwork
- unselfishly helping others

These things happen as we get to know ourselves and become our best versions of ourselves. We find strategies and create habits rather than throwing our hands up and saying we have no control. You have influence over how you spend your day!

We have covered quite a bit of information around our paradigms, safety, and productivity. I have mentioned how personality traits factor into our decisions, behaviors, actions, and results. In the next chapter, let's explore the nine specific personality types and how using Enneagram personality tests can provide valuable insight into building our *safely productive* mind-set.

CHAPTER 5
PERSONALITY TYPES AND DEVELOPMENT

As part of the process of building a healthy balance between safety and productivity, and becoming more engaged and satisfied in work and in life, we will introduce you to a personality trait testing program called the *Enneagram*.

With its roots in ancient Greece, the Enneagram provides a nine-by-nine system that provides us with the tools to become more self-aware about the behaviors that subconsciously drive us to act in certain ways. There are nine distinct personality types. When you complete the Enneagram test, you will see your personality type, and in many cases, you will have characteristics of additional types as well.

The Enneagram can help us become more accountable. It can help us understand why we sometimes find ourselves acting and feeling like victims. Being a victim is self-defeating and makes us feel powerless in making real positive change. We may go to work every day feeling like life is happening *to us* instead of *taking responsibility* and actively engaging in our own journeys.

The more we understand what motivates us, the more we can use these motivations to our benefit and overcome any challenges so we can begin to live a more enriched life.

In this chapter, we will talk about the nine Enneagram personality types and the nine levels of development. Much of what you will read here is based on research provided by the Enneagram Institute. The use of Enneagram personality types helps us understand who we are at a deeper level and see what motivates us and drives us. It also helps us see what we can achieve when we focus on moving up the levels of development (more on this later).

The Nine Personality Types

Many years of research tell us that we all emerge from childhood with *one* of the nine types dominating our personalities. This largely determined how we learned to adapt to our early childhood environment. By the time we were four or five years old, our consciousness had developed enough that we developed a sense of self. Although our identities were still forming at that age, we established ourselves and found ways of fitting into the world. Paradigms and worldviews were being developed. You will see the nine personality types below and a brief description of each. Keep in mind that these are just highlights and do not represent the full spectrum of each type.

The Enneagram Personality Types

Type 1: Reformer. Principled, orderly, perfectionist and self-righteous.

Type 2: Helper. Caring, generous, possessive, and manipulative.

Type 3: Achiever. Ambitious image-conscious, adaptable, and hostile.

Type 4: Individualist. Intuitive, expressive, self-absorbed, dramatic, and depressive.

Type 5: Investigator. Perceptive, original, knowledge-seeking, detached, and eccentric.

Type 6: Loyalist. Committed, engaging, defensive, loyal, paranoid, and devil's advocate.

Type 7: Enthusiast. Enthusiastic, accomplished, uninhibited, manic, and scattered.

Type 8: Challenger. Self-confident, decisive, dominating, and combative rule-breaker.

Type 9: Peacemaker. Peaceful, reassuring, empathic, complacent, neglectful, and avoidant.

There are many different personality types and combinations that we come across in our industry and at various levels of development. I encourage you to go online and find out what your Enneagram type is on the Enneagram Institute website at www.enneagraminstitute.com.

The Enneagram Institute provides a detailed report on both the personality test as well as the levels of development for your specific personality traits. There are applicable fees for the Enneagram personality test, but it is an excellent test, and the written report is a useful tool to use when you are planning your day and week.

I recommend using the Rheti test on the Enneagram Institutes website. It can also be found at www.enneagraminstitute.com. Below are also some more free Enneagram test websites:

- Enneagram Academy: https://enneagramacademy.com/enneagram-test/questions.php
- Eclectic Energies: https://www.eclecticenergies.com/enneagram/test
- The Enneagram Test: https://enneagramtest.net/
- Nine Types: https://enneagramtest.net/

I will caution you ahead of time by telling you that you may not like the result you get—mostly because you may already recognize the traits in yourself and know they are true for you. It's not always easy looking at ourselves this way, exposed and vulnerable, but I will assure you that with knowledge comes great power to do remarkable things.

Now, let's learn more about the nine personality types.

Type 1: The Reformer (Perfectionist)

I have had the good fortune of knowing and working with people in construction with personality type 1: the reformer. They are interesting, hardworking, and constantly strive to be good and right. Their whole self-image is based around this need. They would be well advised to remember that being right needs to be checked. If I believe I am right, I'm using my paradigms to determine what's right and wrong. If my paradigm—the lens I see the world through—is cracked or needs correcting, am I actually right? Paradigm checks are so critical for keeping us on the straight and narrow.

Reformers set such high expectations for themselves and others that it can be disappointing to them when those high standards are not met. Reformers are just as hard on themselves as they are on other people. If you're working with the reformer, and they are hard on their coworkers and seem to hold them at impossibly high standards, you can be sure that internally they are holding themselves to that same level of expected excellence and will continuously pick apart their own actions just as much as the actions of others.

Reformers can become extremely resentful if they see others not working as hard as they are and being rewarded. They don't appreciate anyone getting a free ride. In fact, it's one of the things that aggravates them the most.

Reformers feel the most authentic when they are making an effort and when they are working toward the goal of building a better world. They spend their days focused on making positive change and do not like others breaking their attention or trying to redirect their efforts. Remember, after all, they are trying to change the world. Reformers do well when they accept that perfection is possible; however, they have to learn to accept that there will always be imperfections. They must reconcile that fact. When they do, they can find perfection in so many areas of their lives and let go of the things they can't change.

- Basic Fear: Being seen as bad, wrong, or defective.

- Basic Desire: To be good and be seen as righteous moral, courageous, and honorable.

Development Opportunities for Reformers

- Learn to relax and take time to regenerate and rest your mind. You spend a good deal of your day trying to change the world, and you need to rest.
- Be aware that you tend to become critical of others. Remember that they also take things seriously; they may just take a different approach than you do.
- Learn and create a habit where you accept people as who they are. Set realistic expectations for yourself and others.
- Let your wisdom be your guide. Check your paradigms when trying to decide what the right path is.
- Teach others what you know and be patient with them. Not everyone learns the way you do.

Type 2: The Helper

Personality type 2, the helper, can be seen as emotionally needy. Helpers know how to love and care for the needs of others. They are tender, empathic, and sympathetic, *but* it always comes with a price. Helpers repress their own needs to the point that they don't know what their own needs are. If you ask them, their eyes may well up because they don't know—and they feel ashamed for having any at all.

Their actions tell the world that their only need is to meet yours, but at some point, they will realize that all they have been doing is giving, and nobody is giving back. When this happens, they become angry and resentful and can lash out. They have a great deal of guilt for wanting to be recognized for all they do, and they can dish out the guilt right back with a vengeance. After they have gone away and recovered, they will come back in full helper mode until the cycle repeats itself.

Helpers have a way of anticipating people's needs. They have worked this skill for most of their lives. Sometimes they get in trouble when they do things for others that weren't asked for or expected. A helper may do something for you that you didn't need or even want and become resentful if you don't acknowledge their sacrifices and efforts.

Helpers can be easily manipulated when you talk about what they need. By acknowledging their feelings that no one appreciates them and by telling them what they need to do to change that, they will likely run out and do exactly what you have suggested. As relatively easy as it is to manipulate helpers, be aware that they can become manipulative to get the recognition they have been denied.

- Basic Fear: Being unwanted, unappreciated, and unloved.
- Basic Desire: To feel loved.

Development Opportunities for Helpers

- Learn to connect with your own feelings and needs. Understand that you can live a more fulfilled life by taking care of yourself. There is nothing wrong with caring for yourself first. In turn, you will be better able to love and support others.
- Don't expect to be loved and valued by meeting others' needs. Because you give so much of yourself, you may not always find that it's appreciated. Just because they don't appreciate or acknowledge you, it doesn't mean that you have no value. You may be doing things for people just to be liked.
- Love yourself and others unconditionally for who they are.

Type 3: The Achiever

While I admire the achievers, I also have empathy for them because achievers don't believe they will be loved and accepted unless they are producing a product and turning it over. For them, it's all about the product, result, image, and being seen as competent, successful, and attractive.

Achievers have a lot of energy and can accomplish a lot. They have the ability to organize efficiency and get projects going. They can also recognize talents in others and use those talents to produce. They work long hours and never seem to get tired when they're focused on something that they believe will be valuable and successful. They are natural leaders and know how to please a crowd.

One of the primary reasons this personality trait emerges is that at least one parent's love was conditional and was based on the child's ability to do or produce something.

Achievers grow up when they enter the workforce. They look competent and confident, yet they suffer from enormous self-doubt. When they enter a room, they are subconsciously trying to find ways to impress others by figuring out what they want and by creating a product to serve that need. They also tend to get wrapped up in titles and roles and get security from an impressive position.

They are ambitious, and when they are focused on attaining a goal, they are not above using people in order to achieve that goal. They can be deceitful and can tell a lie and make it sound like the truth.

At the end of the day, an achiever needs one good person who loves them for who they are: the good, the bad, and the ugly. This person provides a safe place for the achiever to be who they are without titles, images, or expectations to constantly produce.

- Basic Fear: Being worthless.
- Basic Desire: To be successful.

Development Opportunities for Achievers

- Slow down. You must take time to recharge yourself physically and emotionally.
- Learn to appreciate the feelings you have and be honest with yourself about your achievements.

- Give admiration to others, practice modesty, and strive to be gracious.
- Don't be afraid of failure. Some of humanity's biggest successes have risen from the ashes of crushing failure.

Type 4: The Individualist

Individualists are known for their conflicted hearts. They feel their emotions intensely, and they try to connect themselves to something beautiful. Individualists are attracted to beauty, and they strive to create a visually appealing environment to live and work in. They have a desire to be authentic and to be seen as one of a kind. There are many impediments to this, and the beautiful things that are created usually come out of great suffering.

When they are unhealthy, they become self-absorbed and can't be bothered by what's going on in the external world. They are dark and moody and can be difficult to live and work with. At their worst, they are prone to suicide. They can sink into depression when they don't feel they are being seen as unique. A lot of shame comes out of these feelings. Others may see them as wonderful and beautiful, but it doesn't matter. The only thing that matters is the internal, depressing dialogue going on in their minds.

They refuse to be one of the crowd, and the thought of being ordinary is a tragedy. There is no energy in being ordinary. The individualist's energy comes from thinking outside the box, seeing the world and its problems differently, and never doing the same task the same way twice.

They can find fulfillment by channeling their drive to create beauty into the things they can influence by finding a meaningful cause where their gifts can shine and bring beauty to the lives of others. Most importantly, they must find contentment in the ordinary.

- Basic Fear: That they have no identity or personal significance.
- Basic Desire: To find their identity and their significance.

Development Opportunities for Individualists

- Learn to always appreciate what is positive in life.
- Accept yourself as lovable.
- Be careful not to pay too much attention to your feelings and your need to have a unique identity.

Type 5: The Investigator

The investigator can be described as the absentminded professor, and they live their lives taking in data. They can often be found at the back of the room, not in a position where they will be engaged, and they can watch and take in the information being discussed.

They are secretive and do not like to discuss themselves. They like to discuss their theories and will often bore their friends and family (they have the idea they are boring because they don't have a strong ability to detect emotional responses from others).

They think their way through life and often report that they feel empty and the need to collect information to fill the void. They are also often loners. They generate their energy from within and can withdraw almost completely. They enjoy seclusion and try to avoid crowds and large gatherings.

Unhealthy investigators can be draining to be around because they may hound others on their team with endless questions and want more and more of your knowledge.

On the other hand, investigators make exceptional counsels. If they are to provide counsel to parties in dealing with an emotional or volatile issue, they are able to remain objective and talk about the data rather than how someone is feeling. They are often the power behind the crown.

Healthy activities for investigators include becoming more engaged with others by connecting their heads and their hearts. They may consider some kind of community service of volunteer work.

- Basic Fear: Being useless, helpless, or incapable.
- Basic Desire: To be capable and competent.

Development Opportunities for Investigators

- Try to calm down in healthy ways. Exercising will help burn off that extra energy and tension.
- Learn to identify situations where your intense involvement in projects is hurting your self-esteem.
- It can be hard to trust others, but don't be afraid to share your feelings. You may find it helpful and very rewarding to have confidants.
- Learn to take more constructive action and move forward into life more fully.

Type 6: The Loyalist

The loyalist craves security and is often filled with fear when they are without leadership they trust. Some say that loyalists make up almost 50 percent of the population and are divided into two subtypes:

The Phobic 6

The Phobic 6 is lovely, naturally humble, teachable, hardworking, and loyal. They make wonderful partners and colleagues. Once they find someone they trust, they will be loyal to the end. However, if the trust is gone, they will leave the relationship in search of something that will provide that much-needed sense of security. These qualities and actions are all still coming from a place of fear.

The Counter Phobic 6

The Counter Phobic 6 can be dangerous because they are filled with immense fear, but they hide it by using bluster and boasting, giving others the impression that they are in control and not experiencing fear. In their worst form, they can become sociopathic and cause a lot of harm, especially when they see themselves as strong leaders who lend their loyalty. They are often attracted to the military lifestyle and have a fascination with guns. They don't want you to see the fear in their eyes, and they worry that others will spot that their natural authority and leadership quality is missing.

Experts say that the loyalist personality emerges from childhood when they felt fear due to very little stability, structure, and organization in the home. This brings about their need for structure, organization, and clear, trustworthy leadership. They value planning and are very good at it.

To move forward, loyalists must find a way to believe in their own authority and ability to lead themselves. They must find a way to trust in themselves and get security from within. The healthy loyalist has all the qualities to do that.

- Basic Fear: Being without support and guidance.
- Basic Desire: To have security and support.

Development Opportunities for Loyalists

- Move forward by learning to trust yourself and find a sense of security by using your gifts of loyalty, humility, and courage.
- Learn to use your anxiety and come to terms with it. Everyone experiences anxiety, and there is nothing unusual about it. If properly used, anxiety can be energizing.
- Learn to notice your preoccupation with danger and projection, become your own authority, and develop greater trust in yourself and others.

Type 7: The Enthusiast

The enthusiast wants to express life to the fullest and doesn't want to miss a thing. When healthy, they engage in fun, thrill-seeking activities because they want to make the world a better place. They love adventures and travel. They are natural optimists and will deny their dark side by avoiding talking about it or dealing with it. Their ultimate need is to be free.

When they are unhealthy, pleasure dictates their choices. They can make unwise and unhealthy decisions in the pursuit of feeling good. They run from pain and avoid it all costs. Enthusiasts leave relationships and jobs when they get hard because they don't like to deal with conflict and pain. They can become impulsive and reckless, not thinking about the consequences of their actions. They have mastered denial, and try to make the best of everything in order to avoid the pain life can bring.

- Basic Fear: Being deprived and in pain.
- Basic Desire: To be satisfied and content—and to have their needs fulfilled.

Enthusiasts want to maintain their freedom and happiness to avoid missing out on worthwhile experiences, keep themselves excited and occupied, and avoid and discharge pain.

Growth Opportunities for Enthusiasts

- Observe your impulses rather than giving in to them. Have fun, but try to measure your approach when indulging yourself.
- Learn to listen to other people in your life. You may be pleasantly surprised at all of the wonderful things you can learn, which opens up new, exhilarating experiences.
- You don't need to have what you want this minute. The thing you crave will likely be there tomorrow. If you relax, great opportunities will often come back around again.

43

- Be sure that what you want now will be good for you in the long run. Learning patience will calm you and likely bring you peace. It can also prevent troubles down the road.
- When it comes to your experiences, consider quality versus quantity. Choose experiences that will leave you fulfilled and that will make your mind and heart soar.

Type 8: The Challenger

Oppositional authority gives challengers their energy. They appear hostile and even cruel, but people should not take it personally because it is a way of engaging others. They hate superficiality, and they are very direct. Ultimately, they are afraid of intimacy; instead, they create indirect intimacy.

They love a challenge and think others do too. In a way, they are often trying to form a bond by challenging others. They oppose you and like it when you oppose them back. Inside all of the huffing and puffing is a very gentle soul, but they will only show that soul to people they feel safe with.

They love to expose the powers that be. If they see a senior leader not doing the right thing, they will become extremely dissatisfied and call them out—even to their own detriment.

They hate being vulnerable, and it's important to look and feel powerful. They like to exude authority. They often avoid admitting they are sick or in pain. They are attracted to high-energy sports and activities that push humans to the edge.

The true gift of the challenger is passion, and to get into their circle of respect, challenge back and remember the gentle soul beneath the surface.

- Basic Fear: Being harmed or controlled by others.
- Basic Desire: To protect themselves (to be in control of their own lives and destinies).

Challengers want to be self-reliant to prove their strength and resist weakness. They also want to be important in their world, dominate the environment, and stay in control of their situations.

Development Opportunities for Challengers

- Your true power is in your ability to uplift people and inspire them to become better. Take the time to work with people and challenge them while you continue to challenge yourself.
- It's okay to occasionally give in to others. You will realize that the cost is low and can significantly improve relationships.
- Many people in your life love and care about you. Don't succumb to feelings that the world is against you. It's not.
- Remember that you are dependent on those around you. To be truly effective and find balance, treat team members with respect and remind them that success will happen because you are all working together to achieve it.
- Remember that power can be terribly lonely if you are isolated from those around you. It's not the most important thing; you and your relationships are.

Type 9: The Peacemaker

For the peacemaker, life can become too much. When that happens, they tend to check out. Peacemakers suffer from a lack of focus. Their lives are often an exercise in finding the path of least resistance. They are likeable because they roll with the punches. They think they are not important and don't jump in and lead conversations because they believe they don't have anything interesting to say. People don't poke and prod them to participate because they don't give off a lot of energy. They bring calm energy to a room, and they can harmonize others in conflict. After listening and observing, they can bring wisdom and logic back to the group. They are naturally humble, and they don't have big egos to contend with.

They will, however, not be self-motivated. Others may see them or describe them as lazy, but if they have a clear set of priorities and processes, they will perform beautifully. They need a structured, scheduled life and can be quite successful in that environment.

Peacemakers are receptive, reassuring, complacent, resigned, accepting, trusting, and stable. They are usually creative, optimistic, and supportive, but they can also be too willing to go along with others to keep the peace. They want everything to go smoothly and be without conflict, but they can also tend to be complacent, simplifying problems and minimizing anything upsetting. They typically have problems with inertia and stubbornness. At their best, peacemakers are indomitable and all-embracing. They can bring people together and heal conflicts.

- Basic Fear: Loss and separation.
- Basic Desire: To have inner stability and peace of mind.

Peacemakers want to create harmony in their environments to avoid conflict and tension, to preserve things as they are, and to resist whatever would upset or disturb them.

Development Opportunities for Peacemakers

- Practice exerting yourself and forcing yourself to pay closer attention to what is going on. Focusing your attention will help you stay present.
- Exercise often. It will increase your awareness and teach you to concentrate.
- If you are having trouble in a key relationship, examine how your own tendencies may have contributed. This may be difficult as the relationship is likely extremely important to you and the feelings you have for others plays a big role in your identity.
- Understand your tendency to go along with others. Doing what others want just to keep the peace may leave you feeling empty

and unfulfilled. Remember to observe your own feelings when moving ahead.

The Nine Levels of Development

Each personality can operate at multiple levels, and these are called *levels of development*. The levels of development show us how personality patterns can change.

You have probably noticed that people change constantly—sometimes they are clearer, freer, more grounded, and more emotionally available, but at other times, they are more anxious, resistant, reactive, emotionally volatile, and less free.

Understanding the levels makes it clear that when people change states within their personalities, they are shifting within the spectrum of motivations, traits, and defenses that make up their personality types.

Each of us can experience times in our lives when we are high functioning and healthy. We feel liberated, happy, and content, and we enjoy healthy, reciprocal relationships. We need balance and contentment. This is typically when we are at our best, and we are at a level of development in level 1–3. Our job is to look for growth opportunities that will help us stay in the healthy development range (level 1–3).

However, we don't always operate like well-oiled machines. Often, we behave "normally." When we still feel some unbalance, we can be a bit controlling and even manipulative at times. We are not always aware, and these things are often done unconsciously. When we feel stress, we can become defensive and have conflict with others. When we experience this, we are operating at development level 4–6. It's normal, but look for those growth opportunities to move up to the 1–3 level.

When we are operating in the development range 7–9, our behaviors will deteriorate to the point where we are at risk of becoming pathological, self-defeating, and destructive. If you are here, I implore you to talk to someone who can help you find a path out. This is an extremely unhealthy place for you, and there is help available to get you moving in the right decision. All is not lost, but intervention is needed.

The following chart depicts these levels:

Healthy Levels 1–3		
Level 1	Feelings of joy, contentment, liberation, and freedom	These behaviors indicate you are high functioning (safely productive)
Level 2	Performing as your ideal self, being happy	
Level 3	Socially capable, performing well in groups	
Average Levels 4–6		
Level 4	Feeling unbalanced, increased defensiveness	These are normal behaviors for your personality type.
Level 5	Looking to control others, manipulative	
Level 6	Overcompensating/having conflicts with others	
Unhealthy Levels 7–9		
Level 7	Being in survival mode	These are severely dysfunctional behaviors for your personality type, and intervention by a professional is advised.
Level 8	Delusional/risk of significant personality disorder	
Level 9	Pathological and destructive	

In the upcoming chapters, we are going to look at some case studies of various members of a construction team, all with different personality types, and see what has helped them move to a *safely productive paradigm.*

I've tested and interviewed engineers, tradespeople, construction and project managers, superintendents, general foremen, owners, and executives from both the contractor side and the owner side. I have selected a handful of stories to share with you, and with their permission, the people have agreed to share their stories to illustrate how their personalities influence their lives.

As you read their stories and gain a better understanding of how their personalities influenced their decisions, make some notes on how you may use your individual strengths to promote the culture of being *safely productive.*

CHAPTER 6
JEFF: THE PIPEFITTER

Enneagram Test Scoring

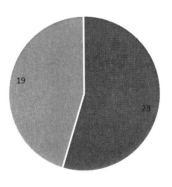

19

23

■ Type 2 Individualist   ■ Type 5 Investigator

When I look back on my years of working projects, so many wonderful memories come flooding back. I think of the challenges and success I have seen teams face. When I think about Jeff, I always remember him with a sense of melancholy for the hard life he led and the inner battles he fought.

Jeff was one of twenty pipefitters who were hired to complete a particularly large workload at a project in Sarnia, Ontario. For the most part, the crew was excellent. However, right out of the chute, Jeff had problems with authority, safety, and getting along with other people. Looking back, Jeff needed help and was deeply troubled.

Jeff grew up in an era where if you wanted to stay busy, you needed to produce, and he was largely left to his own devices when figuring out what to do when he was given a task. He did not grow up in an industry where safety was a value, and he pushed hard to get productivity.

Jeff led a difficult life. He worked to take care of his four children, but he struggled through a long recession and took work where he could get it. Between child- and spousal-support payments, he wondered how he would ever make it.

Jeff suffered from alcohol addiction. Frustrated by life, the daily pressures of being the breadwinner, and never quite feeling like he was enough, he looked for solace in pubs or drinking alone in his camp room. He wanted to stop and had tried unsuccessfully at many points in his life. But now, he was withdrawn, angry, and resentful.

One of the things he had no patience for was being told what rules to follow and when to follow them. He felt everything. Every perceived slight and every glance in his direction was a challenge. He would feel the anger growing each day, and it was only doused slightly by alcohol. He believed he could solve his problems in his mind, but he never found a way to get there. There were just too many angry distractions, and he was completely driven by his feelings.

People generally didn't like Jeff. He came off as aloof and arrogant. While he worked at the site, Jeff was involved in a verbal altercation every other day either with a member of the cleaning staff, safety, or other crew members. He was disciplined for a variety of minor infractions and absenteeism.

One afternoon, the crew was assigned to rig and set in a forty-eight-inch pipe spool that was bolted to a valve. The load was expensive, heavy, and awkward, and it required a long lead time if it ever needed to be replaced. They were to set the valve and pipe into position in preparation for hydro-testing the next day. The job was planned meticulously by the piping superintendent and quality assurance. Everyone knew their role, and the work was moving ahead according to plan. Around noon, one of the senior fitters who planned to be on the job went home sick, and the crew was without one of its key members.

Across site, Jeff had just finished his bolt-up job before lunch. Jeff's foreman told the superintendent that Jeff was free to join the rigging team. The superintendent didn't know Jeff that well, but he figured he had been there for a while and seemed to be capable of assisting, so he agreed.

The area was congested, and there was work being conducted in adjacent areas. Structural steel and other materials were close by, making the work area tighter than usual. Jeff was responsible for collecting the rigging, rigging up the load, and then holding the tagline to direct the pipe spool into place while it was on the crane hook.

Jeff left with a list of rigging to collect for the job. When he reached the closest rigging storage container, he found most of what he needed—but not everything. The main rigging storage was across the site, and there was no way he was walking that far to get a bigger sling. Frustrated, he grabbed two shorter, smaller, older slings that would *probably* work. He thought about how this always happens—not enough gear when you need it.

He rigged up his end, and another rigger did the other side closer to the valve connection. All the attention seemed to be on that rigging point because of the center of gravity, and the load was much heavier on the other end.

The crane hoisted the load, and as the load was coming into place, another worker noticed there was no tagline being used—and that Jeff was using his hands to move the load into place. He yelled to have the operator signal stop, and he told Jeff that he needed a tagline. Jeff angrily told his colleague to mind his own business and said that he knew what he was doing. Frustrated with Jeff, the other worker shrugged and signaled for the operator to continue. As the load came in, one of the older slings failed, sending the valve end directly and swiftly toward Jeff, crushing him between stacked structural steel and the vertical valve.

It was quiet for what seemed to be an eternity, and the silence was shattered by the sound of someone yelling, "Man down!"

An ambulance came and took Jeff to the hospital. The project manager, Jeff's foreman, and the site safety coordinator went to the hospital with him and waited for the news. Everyone feared the worst while they waited for the doctor. The worst-case scenario on any work site had very likely just happened, and it was unclear if Jeff would survive.

Five hours after they arrived, they were told that Jeff had three fractured ribs, a fractured wrist, and cuts and bruises, but to everyone's relief, he would recover. The site was shut down for the next three days while the incident was investigated.

Jeff was quiet and didn't want to talk to anyone, including his children who sat vigil at the hospital. What really went on in his head is anyone's guess since he said little in the first two days. On day three, he agreed to provide a statement and was uncharacteristically cooperative. Perhaps he considered all that happened—and that he was given a second chance to look at life and how he had made decisions up to that point.

Shortly after, Jeff received his discharge from the hospital. He packed his things, washed up, and prepared to leave. As he was getting ready, he tripped and fell over a chair in his room, which caused one of his fractured ribs to puncture his lung. He also suffered an additional abdominal injury and started bleeding internally.

Jeff's condition was rapidly deteriorating. The doctor told Jeff's oldest daughter that because of years of alcohol abuse, Jeff had liver cirrhosis. The vessels in his liver were bursting so rapidly that they could not stop it. Jeff died six days after rigging his last load, never getting the opportunity to take that second chance and see where his life may have taken him.

Jeff personality type was type 4, the individualist, and type 5, the investigator.

Jeff's personality is naturally a tortured soul. Individualists feel everything and often use their feelings to guide their decisions and reactions. The problem is that feelings never give the whole picture and are rarely based in fact. Jeff's personality gave way to a wild imagination where he would imagine conversations he should have had, and he fantasized about what he should have said or could have said. He took the happy moments in his life and relived them over and over, hoping to get the happiness back, often unsuccessfully.

Jeff knew his trade very well and could undoubtably find an innovative way to solve almost any problem. He longed to be seen as unique and interesting. Unfortunately, the investigator part of his personality was naturally reclusive, and it was extremely difficult for him to find a place to call home. He was rarely part of a healthy social group.

When working with someone with Jeff's personality characteristics, in order to challenge and motivate them, try the following:

- Try to find ways to bring them about and reengage by involvement and consultation on work execution.
- Ask them what they think about how to do a job and what the safest way is to do it. By drawing on and recognizing their experience, they will start to feel valued and appreciated.
- If there is a substance abuse issue, help them get help through a supportive approach and show them that they will not be abandoned because they are going through a rough spot in life.
- A supervisor may also consider placing them in a position or role where coordination and organization are important, such as tools and equipment management. In Jeff's case, he was quick to see what was wrong, and given an opportunity, he likely would have taken it as a challenge and may have done great things

CHAPTER 7
WADE: THE CONSTRUCTION MANAGER

Enneagram Test Scoring

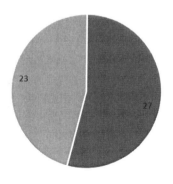

■ Type 9 The Challenger   ■ Type 1 The Reformer

One of the coolest people I have ever met was Wade. I worked with him on a two-year project, and there was never a dull moment. His crew loved him, but the senior management sometimes struggled with him.

He was the definitive challenger, and he liked to call out those he didn't feel were giving the project the support it needed.

The work scope, the schedule, and the budget were closely managed under Wade's watchful eye, and he expected that the crew aligned themselves to a simple expectation: that safety was an unwavering condition of employment.

Wade was hilarious and just plain fun to be around—unless you disagreed with him. If you did, he was tough. He firmly believed in doing the right thing, and he had no patience for wishy-washy managers and executives who had problems with making decisions. He was at every safety meeting, front and center. He was always in charge, and he never shied away from his responsibilities. Wade enjoyed taking on challenges as well as giving others opportunities that challenged them to exceed. He was charismatic and had the required capacities to persuade others to follow him into all kinds of endeavors from starting a company, to rebuilding a city, to waging war, to making peace.

His sense of mission led him to want to improve the world in various ways, using whatever degree of influence he had. He wanted to make a difference. He strove for excellent performance—even at the cost of immense sacrifice. When I spoke to him about what it took to become *safely productive*, as usual, he was very clear and concise.

Wade came from a construction family and had a long history of working and leading major projects. He was proud of his dad, a leader in the industry, and his dad was proud of him. Wade was a chip off the old block. Wade's dad was highly skilled, capable, and competent. He traveled to many countries and worked on many complex large-scale projects.

Wade completed his education at thirteen different schools over the years in construction. His dad traveled for work, and the family went with them. Ironically, Wade vowed to never work in construction, but after all the upheaval at home to accommodate his dad's work, he felt that it was just too disruptive to the family.

When construction folks came by the house, they were always held in the highest regard. Wade saw them as highly intelligent, articulate people who were worthy of his respect. He admired the way they spoke openly and carried themselves with dignity.

Despite his earlier vows to do something else, he continued his education and followed his dad right into the industry. He completed a civil engineering technologist program, and by the time he was twenty-seven, Wade was a superintendent.

In many ways, Wade's dad was ahead of his time when it came to matters of safety. From the time Wade was very young, he was told about how critical safety was on a jobsite, and without it, you have nothing.

Wade recalls his dad telling him a story about a project he was on that budgeted for four fatalities. There were four general foremen (GF) on the job. That was one fatality per GF. Things were turbulent on the job, and despite efforts to keep things under control, incidents and injuries seemed to spiral out of control. Nothing he said seemed to be making a difference.

Wade's dad, desperate to turn things around, called in his GFs. When they arrived, he pulled out the time sheets, showed them all the names, and said, "Pick four people because the way we're going, we're going to kill people."

The general foremen looked confused and obviously could not pick four names from their time sheets. To be asked to identify the human being who wouldn't go home to their family left a profound impression on those leaders. After the shock wore off, they began to collaborate and openly discuss the challenges they were facing as a team.

Wade's dad took extreme measures to make it personal enough for the leaders on his team. With a commitment and a solid plan to move ahead, they finished the job—and never had to use the "fatality budget."

The first time Wade was put in charge of a crew, his challenger personality emerged. Wade remembered all the learnings from his dad and tried to take them with him. He remembered the respect he had for the tradespeople he met when he was younger, and he set out to always treat them with the dignity and respect they were entitled to.

As a young man in charge of tradespeople—who were often much older and more experienced than him—proved to be difficult. The tradespeople challenged him, and he challenged them right back. If they would not comply with the safety requirements, the answer was easy: "Replace them."

Shortly into the project—and after Wade had terminated more than a few workers—he fired someone who was well respected and admired by the crew. The crew knew where to hit Wade where it hurt, and they put down their tools and headed for the lunchroom. They had enough of this guy and his approach to forcing his rules on them. Wade was scared shitless.

The project manager didn't know what had happened and why Wade's entire team was at a complete standstill. So, with his hard hat in his hand, he went to the trailer to speak to them. He talked openly and honestly with the crew about what it meant to him each time someone was injured. He spoke about how personally he took their safety and how he couldn't fathom what it would do to him if he had to speak to someone's family and try to explain that he had a chance to save their loved one but didn't. He told them there was a list of things in his life that he was not prepared to do, and that was number one.

He noticed that the crew understood, and some of the members nodded in agreement. The crew went back to work, and Wade had a paradigm shift: "You can't fire everyone who disagrees with you, but you can be open and honest and give them the best information you can to help them make the best decisions they can." Wade's approached changed, and he grew as a leader, finding great satisfaction in work and seeing people succeed.

Wade's personality type was type 8, the challenger, with additional personality traits of type 1, the reformer.

Challengers have an abundance of willpower and vitality. They feel large and alive when they are exercising these talents. They use their energy to leave their mark and make a lasting positive change in the environment, but they also use their gifts to keep people from hurting themselves and those they care about.

Challengers are rugged and stand alone. They want to be independent, and they resist being indebted to anyone. They often refuse to be politically correct and don't care if people like it or not. They move forward and often inspire others. They know they won't make everyone happy, and they accept that. They are willing to live with those consequences and use that determination to make the world better for all.

When they feel pressure and stress, they are at risk of becoming controlling, self-important, confrontational, and territorial. They may respond by throwing their weight around. They do this to get people in line and regain their sense of control and security.

At their best, challengers naturally have a resourceful, can-do attitude. They take the initiative and make things happen with passion. They are honorable, authoritative, and natural leaders who have a solid, commanding presence. Being so grounded helps them with decisiveness.

Wade shared some of the strategies that he found most effective when trying to influence a shift to a *safely productive* mind-set with his teams:

- The crew is a mirror image to their leadership. If a supervisor stands up in a meeting and talks about their commitment to safety, but then goes out into the field yelling, throwing their weight around, and forcing people to follow their rules, the crew will respond by becoming belligerent and retaliatory. They may work safely only for compliance, and they may choose to slow things down to a crawl to show that you can have safety, but productivity will be a distant memory. Never send mixed messages. Your actions must mirror your words, and by doing so, you build trusting and collaborative relationships with your team.

- When an incident happens, don't let things fester. If you need to make a hard decision to terminate because the infraction was a flagrant disregard of a safety process, then do it. Be fair, firm, and consistent. Always. If you have put in the hard work in building the trust of your team, they will understand and support you. If someone is well intentioned and is trying to do the right thing, before they go home, let them know that you will talk with them tomorrow and ask them to focus on what "we, together" can do to prevent a reoccurrence. Don't let them go home wondering about their fate and be fearful. When someone is in this frame of mind, they can spend the night dreaming up all types of unhealthy things. Some people think, *Let him stew for a while.* Wade disagrees. By letting the person know that you are committed to working through the challenge with them, it further demonstrates your commitment to them. Additionally, if you do have to suspend someone, when they return, make a point of stopping by to check on them. They need to know that grudges aren't being held, that their debt is paid, and that it's all about moving forward together. The first visit may be awkward, so be sure to follow up with a second, so they know the commitment is real.

- Projects, from time to time, experience a wave of incidents. Things like objects falling from heights can put a scare into any worker and their leader, and when you have five of these events in a week, it's hard not to take serious action to stop the trend. First of all, take the incidents seriously and engage the members of your team to find smart and safe ways to correct the problem. Don't go overboard and impose strict, unachievable rules punishable by a night in the stockade. They won't work, and they won't stick. Once the hysteria has passed, they will go back to doing what they always did. Instead, look at the root/ core causes and find smart, reasonable action to correct the condition. There are so many changes to equipment, processes, and technologies. Use them as opportunities to bring out their most innovative nature. They will bring their best ideas to the table, and you may just come up with an innovation that changes the industry, is safe, and improves productivity. Don't let the opportunity to further engage your team pass you by.

- Finally, remember that being *safely productive* starts and ends with the people. Powerful leaders will open their hearts to their crews. A crew can pick out a phony with the accuracy of a Special Forces sniper. To build trust with the crew, you must be willing to show them where they are vulnerable. Be honest and open about what's going on—and sincerely invite their involvement in tackling any problem that the team may encounter. Just as it was with the construction folks who used to visit at Wade's house, he still believes the crew is worthy of respect and must be treated with dignity.

When working with Wade's personality traits, one may consider the following suggestions to keep the challenger and reformer engaged and performing at their best:

- We must always strive to work to the highest ethical standard. The reformer part of Wade's personality demanded that he always do the right thing. By providing ethical leadership to people with reformer characteristics, you will be pulling the best parts of their personality to the forefront, and they will staunchly defend you, your project, and your team with all they have. If anyone suspects that hidden agendas are at play and that people are treated poorly, the reformer will retract and likely lose faith in the project leadership.

- A clear, compelling purpose must exist for people like Wade. Share the big picture with people with this personality type. They will understand, and they will help move the needle toward a successful outcome. Give them as many details as you can, and they will bring their best efforts forward. People need to know what they're doing, why they're doing it, and what value it brings. Many workers don't know what they're doing past the first coffee break, and they certainly don't understand how they fit into the big picture.

- A signal that it's time to do a little digging is if Wade were to become highly critical of himself and others. If this happens, it's time to engage and listen. Remind them that being too critical is not fair to the people who are there trying to do their job.

Challenge them to become part of the solution and not to be too hard on everyone, including themselves, which can bring down the morale of everyone else. The reformer and challenger will step up to the challenge.

The challenger will defend what's right, and they will do so with passion and in the face of risk to themselves. I'm thankful for having the opportunity to work with a leader of Wade's caliber, and each day, I witnessed the strongest attributes of his personality emerge while he focused on paving the way for each of us to be *safely productive.*

CHAPTER 8
CURTIS: THE MILLWRIGHT

Enneagram Test Scoring

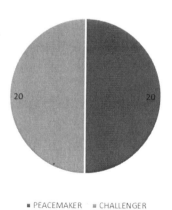

20   20

■ PEACEMAKER   ■ CHALLENGER

I started working with Curtis around the same time that I became an executive for the first time. I had always been around very strong, capable construction people. I took pride in the fact that I had been mentored by some of the best, and I believed I had found a good balance between firm and fair, and consistent and compassionate, until I met Curtis.

Curtis put his boots on every day and came to work. He was there early making coffee and planning his day. The early risers were there to get some quiet time, and they would take full advantage of the silence of the phone or the absence of someone in their doorway with a question. However, Curtis always seemed to take the approach that the biggest part of this planning involved talking with the people he would be working with that day. He would do so in a calm, caring, compassionate way, and he was sincerely interested in hearing what the members of his team were thinking and feeling. Sitting and talking with Curtis reminded me of sitting in someone's kitchen with a hot cup of coffee, in the caring ear of somebody who never made you feel like they had someplace better to be.

Curtis was raised in a very close family where he always had access to a parent. His dad, a mechanic by trade, worked for the Department of Highways. He was at work a lot, but when he wasn't, Curtis and his brothers were with their dad—either spending time on the water or puttering around and tinkering on some project around the house. Curtis had a wonderful childhood. He was always outside running, playing, or building a fort with his brothers, and he remembers being part of a big, welcoming, and caring family.

Curtis wasn't the kind of person to get into trouble. He always felt there were too many sets of eyes holding him accountable. Getting in trouble and having to answer to this big family wasn't the kind of hassle that he needed or wanted. Like most of us, Curtis was no angel, but he never did anything where trouble followed him home.

When he was a very young man, he considered a career in law enforcement, but he knew that the wait times were far too long, and he needed to work. He always had a passion for building and changing the landscape. He always loved the time he spent with his dad building and fixing things, so when he spoke to an industrial mechanic, the thing that resonated with Curtis was that no two days would be alike in construction.

He completed his apprenticeship and became a journeyman in the nineties. That was a time when safety wasn't at the forefront of either management or workers. Basic PPE (personal protective equipment) was a set of coveralls and work boots, and if you wore those things, you were complying.

Early in his career, he was working in a plant on rotating equipment in some very congested areas. Almost every day, he would go home with a goose egg on his head from ducking to get out of the way of some falling material. He and his crew asked the managers to order some bump hats, and while the plant operators thought it was hilarious, they thought it was the best thing to do. No more goose eggs. It wasn't mandatory, but it seemed like the smart thing to do, so they did it.

Curtis and his crew worked in many different areas in various plants, and they sometimes found themselves in risky situations like working at heights with no protection. They worked anyway, and they didn't *really* think there was anything wrong with it. They understood that risk came with the job, and they took the risk without actually questioning it. They just tried to do the right things. To them, safety was about self-preservation, and they took care of each other.

Around 2000, Curtis noticed a shift in how companies looked at safety. They were starting to look at safety as a means of self-preservation, and they were seeing the changes in legislation around the worker's expectation for safer workplaces. Companies were beginning to realize that injuries and incidents would no longer be tolerated to the degree that they had been.

The 2000s were a decade of change. Curtis worked in environments where safety was critically important to owners, and money was spent to ensure that the workers went home safely. None of this was a shock to Curtis since he had always believed in working safely, but this time, there were resources and commitments from the decision-makers.

Curtis's personality type was type 9, the peacemaker, and with additional characteristics of type 1, the challenger.

Healthy peacemakers are easygoing and emotionally stable. They are open and unselfconsciously serene. They are known to be trusting and patient with themselves and with others. Their openness allows them to be at ease, and as a result, others find it very easy to be in their company. Healthy peacemakers like Curtis want to believe the best about other people, and they hope for the best in themselves. Crew members enjoy working and talking with them, and having a nine on their team. People find comfort and seek counsel from nines when they need to be reminded that life is not about personal gains or winning. It's about everybody feeling a sense of inclusion and accomplishment and leaving the job each day feeling like they are part of something that mattered.

When peacemakers find themselves in conflict, it threatens their comfort and peace of mind, and they are at risk of becoming complacent or disengaged. They can become worried, frustrated, and angry about being put into that position. They will look for ways to regain their independence. When exposed to prolonged conflict and stress, they find comfort in their old habits, puttering around and finding different types of work to keep their minds busy. By doing this for long periods, they avoid making decisions and brush problems under the rug. They may even spend a lot of their time thinking about the good old days. If someone tries to reengage them, they may become passive-aggressive and stubborn to resist people who are trying to bring them back.

When peacemakers get down in the dumps, they can resign themselves to the fact that nothing can be done to improve their situations. They look for magical, easy solutions, and they keep waiting for their ship to come in without any effort on their part—and they may wait a very long time.

At their best, they feel autonomous and fulfilled because they live in the moment and are true to themselves. They have profound relationships, are intensely alive, and are fully connected to themselves and others. What a great person to have on the team. Curtis was just that type of person.

Curtis shared a time in his career when he felt his independence being threatened. His belief and need to do the right thing were so threatened that he left the project site determined to leave it all behind. He was not prepared to let it go and get along even if it meant peril for him, and so, the challenger emerged. When he was later contacted to return, like the true peacemaker he was, he agreed and was able to resolve the challenges he faced earlier.

During Curtis's progression into a leadership role, I had the privilege of witnessing one of the greatest leaders emerge who I had ever seen. When Curtis talked openly and with true sincerity about the role that leaders must play, I felt like I was back in Curtis's kitchen. He said, "It starts with how workers are hired."

Active involvement in reading resumes and interviewing potential workers is a valuable way to recruit people with the *safely productive* mind-set. Leaders don't always get involved in this process, but it's critical that they use their experience and their expectations to start the process of setting new workers up for success.

Managers and frontline leaders must have a clear and consistent message that they expect safe and productive work and put the process, tools, and leadership in place to support this goal. The environment that the workers come into must be set up to support and allow safe and productive work. This means conflicting messages from leaders—both verbal and behavioral—must be eliminated, and the worker should never question or waiver on the mind-set of being *safely productive*. He added that, if a client places unrealistic goals on the manager, we must never put ourselves in a position where we overcommit at the expense of safety. We must always be transparent about any scheduling concerns with the client. If we don't have what our team needs to succeed, both safety and productivity will suffer.

He shared a few strategies to help move a crew toward being *safely productive*:

- A crew is going to measure themselves by what they get done in a day. If the leadership holds the trust and respect of the workers, they will work safely *and* productively. Without trust and respect, it's a bit of a crapshoot. If they don't trust the leadership and the message, they may go into self-preservation mode, taking care of each other and themselves. This can result in field decisions being made without all the necessary information to stay safe.
- The people who have done the work are the best resources to tell us how to do the job safely and how long it will take. Their

input must be sought, considered, and implemented into the plan. If there are improvements on how to do the work safely and productively, these can come from both the supervisor and the crew—if they are both willing to listen and respect each other's views.

- If one member of the crew is struggling to find the balance between safety and productivity, they should be mentored one-on-one. It's important to know each member of the crew because when leaders take the time to get to know them as human beings and understand what drives and motivates them both on and off the job, they can help them overcome any challenges they may face. Supervisors always need the courage to be clear and firm on what the safety and productivity expectations are—and not to be bashful about holding people accountable. Most people will work hard to try to do what they've been asked, and if they struggle, the best approach is to bring them in closer to understand their challenges and help them succeed. If workers find themselves unable to strike a balance despite your efforts to mentor, then a hard decision may be required. Maybe this environment is not aligned with the person's values, personality, or level of development, and continuing an unhealthy relationship places everyone at risk. A leader should make no assumptions about what's in a person's heart, and they should make every effort to understand what's going on with the worker so they can help and support them.

- Sometimes an impossible schedule makes a great team. At some point, we all face tight, demanding schedules. When a leader shares the challenges and engages the crew toward being safely productive, they may be surprised at some of the innovative, smart, and efficient ways to achieve both. Tradespeople know there are schedules and deadlines. They should never be used to threaten or coerce people into hurrying, but when used wisely, they can engage, invigorate, and light a fire under the members of the team to contribute and bring new fresh ideas to planning, execution, and safety. None of us can succeed in isolation. We will get the best results when we communicate and work to a common set of core values. A good, safe, and productive crew can accomplish what some would think is impossible.

When working with a personality like Curtis, the following strategies should be considered to keep them operating at their best:

- Don't mess with them. Create a place where they can trust you and feel at peace with the environment they are in. When they can trust their team members, they will be forthcoming and helpful in overcoming most safety- or productivity-related issues. When they are at their best, they will work to find solutions that are a win-win for all if they are given the responsibility to do so.
- When you have a high-pressure schedule, use their skills and traits to keep things calm. They will not escalate things or bring additional pressure to the crew. Try using their talent on a critical piece of the work. Provide all necessary information, and they will alleviate at least part of a stressful project.
- Allow them to have direct interactions with the client or other stakeholders. Their drive to create a winning situation will benefit what could otherwise be a stressful situation.

I left our conversation, as I always did, feeling like I had just spent time with a dear friend. It felt good knowing that Curtis was out there, being Curtis, taking care of the crew in all aspects—with zero harm of any kind. I am grateful that his crew has him—and I'm happy for their families—and that Curtis is looking out for them.

CHAPTER 9
SYLVAIN: THE SUPERINTENDENT

Enneagram Test Scoring

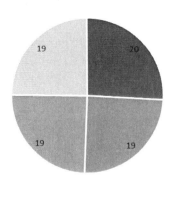

■ HELPER   ■ LOYALIST   ■ INDIVIDUALIST   ■ PEACEMAKER

In 2008, I worked with Sylvain, a millwright superintendent, on a large industrial project in Northern Alberta. Sylvain was very capable and knowledgeable, and he always worked with safety collaboratively. I admired him because of his commitment to safety and his willingness to hold his team accountable. His risk assessments and work plans were always thorough and done well. His level of task detail and strict compliance to policies were beautiful things. When he was asked to take on lockout training (isolating an energy source) and deliver to French-speaking workers, he did so willingly and executed the training flawlessly. I always felt like his crew and his lockout students truly understood it. I was very happy Sylvain was with us.

I thought I had Sylvain figured out. He was an excellent tradesman who embraced safety and shared his knowledge willingly. I figured he had lived a routine life with a good work-life balance. I also assumed that at that stage of his career, he was comfortable enough in his leadership style to work safely *and* productively while leading others in the same direction. I had my head up my ass when it came to Sylvain.

Growing up in a small town in Quebec, Sylvain was raised by two people, who he now says tried their best, but weren't equipped to be parents. Both of Sylvain's parents were raised in abusive environments, and they carried their trauma and patterns of abuse into adulthood and parenthood with them. He had an extremely painful childhood.

Sylvain began working at a young age. Like most kids, his first job was helping out in a local restaurant. He had a good work ethic and liked working with people. He enjoyed staying busy and productive.

His next job was with a printing company. Sylvain was eighteen and worked on the maintenance of the plant's equipment. He recalls a time when he and his crew had to connect welding machines at the electrical panel. There was the panel, but there was also a fully stocked bar. This was when Sylvain started drinking at work. It was common, and everyone was doing it. Nobody, including management, said a thing about it, and life just carried on. As long as they delivered results, everyone looked the other way.

He continued to find work in the mechanical trade industry and soon found himself working at a quarry in downtown Montréal, Quebec. He recalls working at extreme heights many times without any type of fall protection. They had belts available, but nobody used them, and nobody cared. Like the last job he was on, drug and alcohol use was rampant on the work site. Most people were using, everybody knew it, but nothing was ever done or said about it.

Sylvain reminisced about a time where he and a crew of ironworkers were bringing material and equipment up to a tower. Sylvain recalls taking the stairs and bringing rigging with him. When they all arrived at the top of the tower, they smoked a joint and started to work. The supervisors knew that this was routine for the crew, and as before, if they were producing, nothing was ever said, and they were left alone.

By that time, Sylvain was a full-blown addict. One day on the job, he got into a physical altercation with a foreman. They were at the top of the tower and began to argue. When things got heated, Sylvain punched the foreman in the face, causing him to fall down a flight of stairs. The supervisor stumbled to his office and collapsed. At the hospital, they feared he might have suffered a heart attack following the assault. Sylvain was given the choice to walk away or they would call the police. He chose to leave the job, and he never heard anything else about the incident.

When Sylvain was twenty-seven, he worked for a large contractor that was demolishing a factory. The environment was highly hazardous. They had to dismantle galvanized steel structures, tanks, and vessels, which had significant amounts of chemicals. One morning, as they were preparing to enter an extremely hazardous and confined space with life-threatening conditions, the supervisor asked which crew members would be willing to undertake this high-hazard work. Sylvain and another addict raised their hands. They were the only ones. During that period, Sylvain had no regard for his life or his well-being—and neither did the other addict. Sylvain told himself that if he died on the job, then so be it. It was not a bad way to go. Sylvain and the other addicts could always be relied on to take on the most hazardous work because they just didn't care.

He recalled a time when they worked in another tower, hoisting material up using a gin-wheel-type hoist. To protect one other from a fall, one worker would hoist the material up or down while Sylvain held onto his collar with one hand and a handrail with the other. Alcohol and drugs continued to flow through the jobsites, and safety was never taken seriously in any way, shape, or form.

Horseplay and messing around on the jobsite, especially during high-hazard work, was no problem. One day, Sylvain and a coworker were installing rails for an overhead crane without fall protection. He and Maurice decided they would pretend they were fighting while they were very high up to scare the young engineer who was supervising them. When the fake fight began, Sylvain smeared ketchup on his face to make it appear as though he was severely injured in the fight. The two of them threw fake punches and pushed each other as though one was going to throw the other off the structure. Both impaired, it was all a big joke, but the engineer was sufficiently terrified. They all carried on with their work, and nothing more was said.

The closest Sylvain ever came to losing his life was when he was installing a conveyor at another quarry. On that day, since there was no crane operator, one of the millwrights jumped into a 160-ton capacity crane. He tested the controls and believed he could operate it, but he had no formal training or previous experience. Sylvain was positioned at one end with his back to channel iron. The massive conveyor, on an angle, was rigged and hoisted using multiple chain hoists with no lashing of any kind. Sylvain knew the chain hoists on the site were in dire condition. They had been exposed to so much heat, and many of them had been red-hot at times and should have been taken out of service since the integrity of the steel was minimal. Those chain hoists were being used to hoist the conveyor that day.

When the crane began to lower the load into position, one of the hoist chains broke, and the conveyor started to swing. The worker in the crane had no knowledge about how to control the load, and he froze and did nothing but helplessly watch as the load swung. Sylvain was stuck in position at his end and had nowhere to go as the conveyor section swung toward him. At that point, he knew he was going to die when it struck him. He had the presence of mind to know that he was likely going to be cut in half. He had no anxiety or stress at that moment. As before, he had no regard for himself or his life—and he didn't care if he lived or died. He just said, "Goodbye."

To his surprise, the load stopped before crushing him. However, it pinned him in position. When the load came to rest, the supervisor came out and instructed the crew to clean up the area and continue with the work. It was productivity at any cost.

In 1992, Sylvain decided he wanted to live. He stopped using drugs and alcohol, and he slowly found his way back into the world. He became a father, and like most men who find themselves in that position, he had a paradigm shift and made a commitment that he would never abandon his children.

In 2007, Sylvain made his way out west and took a project on Vancouver Island, British Columbia, during the pulp mill shutdown. It was the first time Sylvain participated in a new worker orientation. He was surprised and couldn't believe such a level of safety could be achieved.

That was also the first time Sylvain ever saw a worker terminated for fall protection violation for breaking the plane of the scaffold and placing themselves at risk of a fall. Sylvain had witnessed so many safety infractions over the years and so many cases where people put their lives at risk, but for the first time since he started his career, he saw someone being held accountable. He went back to his crew and warned them that they were taking safety very seriously, and if they wanted to stay on the project, they needed to work safely at all costs.

Now, let's be clear, Sylvain wasn't fully on board with every safety rule he was exposed to, and he thought the termination of the worker was going a bit overboard. However, he accepted that that was the environment he was in and that he and his crew had to work to the expectations of this employer or leave.

Like many others in the mid-2000s, Sylvain found himself on an oil sands facility in Northern Alberta. He was exposed to safety rules, regulations, and processes like he had never seen. Admittedly, he says he thought a lot of it was "bullshit," but one thing was certain: if you couldn't work safely, then you couldn't work there. Therefore, he did what he was told, followed the rules, and stayed safe.

He also watched what the other crews were doing, and he found himself particularly intrigued with a crew of scaffolders. They put on their fall protection equipment, carried their tools, worked at great heights, and built everything from simple structures to scaffolds that would encompass the diameter and height of the massive tower. They did it with such ease and professionalism that it seemed like they had done it all their lives. What left an impression on Sylvain was the fact that they didn't need a supervisor to tell them to work safely. They kept each other accountable to follow the rules and stay safe. Safety was so powerful with them. Sylvain was so impressed by what he saw from the scaffold crew that he carried that example with him to his next project when he was hired as a superintendent.

When Sylvain arrived at his new project, he was greeted by an old friend. Maurice had been the one in the fake fight many years earlier. Maurice was now the mechanical general superintendent. He had been with the company for several projects and had come to know and embrace a safe and productive mind-set during his time. He told Sylvain that there could be absolutely no question in the minds of the crew about safety. They would work safely, or they would go home—and there was no room for negotiation on that point.

Maurice told Sylvain that two things mattered on the project. The first was safety, and there would be no shortcuts or deviations without consequence. The second was that loyalty to the company and its owner was mandatory. Since safety was their highest priority, it now became theirs as well. Sylvain understood Maurice's expectations, and he carried them out.

The crew that came in for the project needed a lot of coaching and teaching since many of them had come from the same environment as Sylvain. They were at a disadvantage because they were coming out of an industry where safety was not a closely held value, and they did not have any exposure to that level of safety. There was not a lot of time to get them on board, so they required close supervision and were held accountable for any deviations from the safety program. They understood this and accepted the conditions if they wanted to stay— and most of them did.

It was simple and clear. If you are safe and loyal, you can stay. If you can't, you won't. There are exceptions—and the choice is yours. That was how Sylvain ran his crew.

Sylvain's personality type was type 2, the helper, with characteristics of type 6, the loyalist. The long and short of it is that helpers need to learn to care for and appreciate themselves before they take care of anyone else. They might deny their own needs, but at the heart of everything, they want to be appreciated for the many efforts they make for the good of others. When they don't feel appreciated, it pisses them off.

Helpers like people, and they will focus a lot of time and energy on helping others become successful by giving a lot of themselves. They feel good when they are helping others succeed and grow. Helpers will try to make good things happen for everyone, but they don't like one-sided relationships. They want connections where the love, care, and respect are mutual, and they are more than willing to do their part. They also don't like being away from their loved ones.

When helpers are at their best, they are sincere and bighearted and have a ton of goodwill and generosity. Because they are so focused on others, they can sense when things aren't right or when others are down and not themselves. They will go out of their way to support them by emphasizing the good things about them, their lives, and their places in the world. Helpers will always make a point of trying to show you how special you are.

Helpers grow by recognizing that you can care for yourself and care for others too. It doesn't have to be one or the other. They will only achieve what they long for if they love and care for themselves first.

The loyalist part of Sylvain's personality (type 6) is displayed prominently at work. By being a detailed, meticulous planner, he tries to prevent any difficulties by seeing potential problems before they occur. Loyalists believe in dealing with problems before they get out of hand. They organize, prioritize, and complete projects flawlessly. They bring reliability and honor to everything they do. Once they make a commitment, they are all in. Like the commitment Sylvain made to Maurice, he carried it out every day and never wavered.

I asked Sylvain about some of the strategies he used to move his workforce toward a safe and productive mind-set. Like the loyalist he is, he simply said, "If you can't work safely, you can't work here."

You have to spend time with people, giving them the information to make the right decisions. You have to inform them of the rules and expectations and make sure they clearly understand. You must hold them accountable to the commitments they make. This must be carried out with consistency and integrity.

This didn't always make Sylvain the most popular among his crew, but Sylvain told me that he learned one very critical piece of information from a wise construction manager. When the construction manager had to discipline or remove a worker for a serious safety infraction, he simply told them, "I would rather you be pissed off at me as you leave the gate than have to take you back to your family and explain to them why they lost you." Sylvain believed this to his very depths and lived with the fact that some of his crew members just didn't like him. He accepted that.

With strong attention to detail and planning, anticipating problems before they arise, the crew can stay focused on their tasks and have a clear understanding of each step that must be carried out to execute the job.

Today, Sylvain is retired. He has found happiness and contentment and gets a great deal of satisfaction from spending time with his wife and being a part of his children's lives. Over the years, Sylvain also made peace with his turbulent childhood, and he now understands that his parents were flawed human beings who were desperately trying to deal with their own trauma during a time when those things weren't openly discussed. Back then, people didn't get help for the problems they had; they just tried to get by in life the best they could. He has forgiven them both.

Sylvain said that he was surprised that he was still alive and that he had lived through it all. He lived anything but a normal, well-balanced life.

Here are some strategies that could be considered when working with personality types like Sylvain:

- Take advantage of the attention to detail and impeccable planning that the loyalist can achieve. When preparing any task, large or small, meticulous planning and execution will bring both safety and productivity. This is a tremendous skill to have on any crew.

- Remember that they crave strong leadership and support. If they feel they are not getting it, they can become dissatisfied and lose faith. Be worthy of their trust. Be ethical, tell the truth, and be realistic about any challenges.
- The helper part of his personality will work tirelessly toward the benefit of others. Allow them to help and coach others on safe *and* productive initiatives.
- The peacemaker personality part of Sylvain craves harmony in the workplace and win-win solutions for all. Allow them to participate in the coordination of activities around planning and safe execution. They will most often work collaboratively with others and seek out solutions that are smart, efficient, and work for all.

Sylvain gave me such incredible insight into the darker side of construction, and I was left somewhat shaken by how bad it was, and still is, in some parts of the industry. I was even more motivated than when I started this project to see it through and bring these stories to the workforce and their leaders—all thanks to Sylvain.

CHAPTER 10
DEAN: THE RODBUSTER

Enneagram Test Scoring

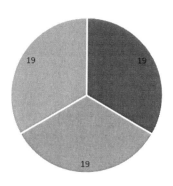

■ CHALLENGER ■ REFORMER ■ ENTHUSIAST

I started working with Dean in 2003 when I went to his project to do some training for the supervisors. I had an absolute blast, and I have never forgotten how much fun we had in that two-day course. It was just the neatest group of supervisors, and I still remember and stay in touch with many of them. The group included Dean, a reinforcing ironworker foreman. Dean was genuinely interested in the safety material, asked a lot of questions, and got along with everyone in the group. When I was interviewing Dean for the case study, I was reminded of what a wonderful person he was. He was always willing to laugh and give you his time.

Dean had an interesting result from his Enneagram test, but if you knew Dean, it was really no surprise. He had a three-way split between the challenger, the reformer, and the enthusiast.

The challenger part of his personality tells us that he is a natural leader. He has an intense desire to hold himself to a high standard and challenge others to excel and be successful. He takes great joy in seeing others on his crew excel and experience the gratification of overcoming a new challenge. When Dean is under pressure or feels like he's losing control, he's the kind of guy who will push back and use his authority to get what he needs. He will tell a member of his crew what he would like done, and if he experiences any unwillingness to follow his directions, his back is likely to go up. He would probably say something like, "Well, thanks for sharing your comments, but go do it."

The reformer part of his personality desperately wants to improve the world. He will put his best efforts toward making things better, and he has little patience for those who he doesn't think are pulling their weight.

The enthusiast part of his personality loves life, new experiences, and being busy working on new and exciting projects. He wants to have choices about how he spends his time, where he spends his time, and with whom he spends his time. He hates being told what to do. To get Dean on board with your plan, you may have to pitch the idea and ask him what he thinks rather than simply saying, "You need to do this."

On the morning I interviewed him, he was in Vancouver, British Columbia. We had coffee over the phone, and what was supposed to be an hour easily stretched into two. I didn't realize how much I had missed him.

Dean told me about his time growing up in southern British Columbia in a beautiful resort town that bordered the United States. In the summer, he always looked forward to the thousands of tourists who would come and the excitement they would bring.

Growing up, Dean had a fantastic time. He was a happy and curious kid who drove his teachers crazy. He asked question after question, and they would get frustrated because they never seemed to be able to get through their lesson plan when Dean was around. He described himself as a *nosy* kid, and he was always a bit of a class clown. He loved to laugh and make others laugh as well. He enjoyed people and life very much.

He spent time with his dad and brother rebuilding hot rods and wanted to be a race-car driver. He loved the energy and adrenaline around the whole scene. His dad would let him ride in the back seat of his car while he raced. Dean would have the time of his life, and it was truly his passion.

Like many in the small town, Dean got his first job making railway ties at the local sawmill. Dean worked on the line where the lumber came out after being stripped to make a specific-sized tie. He worked around conveyors and moving, rotating, and cutting equipment. There was no safety program of any kind, and there wasn't a lot of information given about the equipment, how it operated, and the risks. Dean figured he needed to be alert and watch out for himself. He made sure that he was always on the same page as his partner, and he kept his eyes open.

His crew, for the most part, were ten to fifteen years older than he was, and they were very production driven. If someone screwed up or had an incident, it was funny. They were made fun of, and then they went back to work. If it was serious, they were sent home and replaced. Luckily, Dean never got hurt, but shortly after that, he decided to head off to Calgary, Alberta, to look for work.

He got a job working with a company that specialized in post-tensioning—a process of strengthening concrete by putting tension on the rebar after the concrete is poured. During this time, Dean met a mentor, Wilf, who he would never forget. Wilf was a great big mountain of a man who had a kind heart and time for everyone. Wilf treated everyone with dignity and respect. It was the first time Dean had experienced being treated like an adult and with such kindness in the workplace. After all, he was used to getting laughed at for being careful or for asking too many questions.

Wilf taught him everything he knew about the post-tensioning process, including showing him the drawings and making sure he understood each and every step required to execute the work. There was no safety program or manual to use, but Wilf taught Dean everything he needed to know to stay safe without mentioning the word *safety* once. Dean loved working in this environment. There was an answer for every question he had!

After a couple of years, Dean went to work with his brother and started his rebar apprenticeship. He was lucky enough to find another trainer who held the same values as Wilf: treating people respectfully and giving them all the information they needed to take care of themselves and do a good job so they could be productive and know their jobs inside and out.

At the time, there was no safety on the jobsites: no manuals, no systems, no practices, and certainly no safety coordinators. These folks relied on themselves to know their trade in order to work safely *and* productively. This was not done consciously. There was no discussion about safety or what to do to stay safe. It was all about being productive, and to be productive, you would be trained. And if you were trained, you would be safe.

Dean quickly found out from working in rebar that the crews were small, and workers would often go from job to job with the same people. Having a good group of folks around would make all the difference.

It was common practice for every worker on the site to have a six-pack in their lunch kit. At lunchtime, while the foreman did their paperwork, they could hear beer cans opening all through the trailer. Drug and alcohol abuse was a common problem in the industry at the time, but no one was equipped with a way to deal with it or intervene—and they usually didn't. Jobs went on. Some people would drink six beer before work, work all morning, have six beers at lunchtime, and go out and rig loads, work with cranes, shake out rebar, pour concrete, and erect steel. And if someone was hurt, they never knew about it. The person was just replaced, the mess was cleaned up, and the work continued.

Just to be clear, not everyone was drinking on the job. There were still some who chose to come to work sober, do their jobs, and go home. Those were the kinds of people Dean looked for when he was building a crew.

By that time, Dean was overseeing his own small projects. One particular day, he found out that one of his foremen was drinking with the crew every day. When Dean terminated the foreman, the crew walked off the job. They were outraged that they were not going to be allowed to drink anymore. Dean was so sick and tired of the absenteeism and the belligerent attitudes, and he replaced the entire crew. He was fortunate enough to put a team together that just wanted to do the job, and Dean did his best to do just what his mentors had done: teach them everything they needed to know about their trade and be productive.

One day on the project, the son of the man who owned the company was working on the site. He was shaking out rebar on a structure and was having difficulty pulling apart the rebar. The structure also didn't have a handrail. The rebar down below was exposed and did not have any type of caps or impalement protection. The young man, who was only twenty years old, pulled hard enough on a piece of rebar that when the stored energy released, it sent him back over the edge. He fell twenty-five feet and was impaled on the rebar below. The rebar dowels went through his lungs, and he died on the scene. Twenty years old, with a whole life ahead of him, gone in an instant. The job shut down, and everyone left the site while the police investigated.

The incident affected Dean profoundly. He believed that things needed to change, but he was at a loss about how to bring about meaningful action that would protect workers from those kinds of senseless incidents. There were so many good things about the industry, and he loved what he did, but something was missing. The respect, dignity, and care that he experienced early in his career just weren't there, and they were desperately needed. It was productivity at all costs—and safety was never part of any discussion. Everyone had to take care of themselves. Hopefully, you had a buddy on your crew who would watch your back, and you would watch his.

Dean knew that was just the way things were, but he also knew in his heart that they shouldn't be. To this point, safety was only about instinct and knowing the right thing to do because you knew your trade. The problem was that not everyone knew their trade well, could anticipate, or knew how to plan. Some lacked instinct, were impaired, or just didn't care enough. Whatever the reasons, fatalities continue to happen across the construction industry.

In the early 2000s, there seemed to be an awakening with industrial construction owners that safety was a critical part of any project. A few industry leaders started to budget safety into their projects. Dean also noticed the shift in the workforce.

There also appeared to be an awakening with the workforce in terms of how they viewed safety on the job. In addition, the unions started to take up the cause on the workers' behalf to promote safe work environments. Dean watched all of this with great interest and was hopeful that it would bring about the change that was needed. He also observed that a lot of the people who held the belief that safety rules were silly and worked without regard for themselves and others were retiring or leaving the industry altogether. He thought maybe their lifestyles caught up with them—or they just couldn't make the transition to a stronger safety focus.

The first project he was on, during this transition where safety was a priority, was at a pulp mill in the interior of British Columbia. New worker orientations, fall protection training, confined space entry training, and leadership safety training were happening, and he loved it. The new learning and experiences were exhilarating to his enthusiast personality, and he fully embraced it because he liked the job and knew what they expected of him.

Between 2003 and 2017, Dean worked on some of the largest industrial projects in Western Canada for some of the largest owners. He attributes his progression in his career to embracing a safely productive mind-set. Here's what he has to say:

- Managers, supervisors, and workers need open minds when it comes to following processes and policies. It's not for us to fight and resist. It's our responsibility as tradespeople to understand the rules around our work and follow them. If pilots were to skip steps that they didn't think were necessary, we as passengers would be pissed, and anyone who catches a plane would be at risk. If we don't like the rules, we should find something else to do that we enjoy.

- Owners and clients need to reexamine their ideas of what productivity is. The days where it was production at all costs are gone because the cost to people was too high. The good old days weren't good for people who worked without proper protection or policy to protect them.

- Being safe shouldn't be about carrying all the blame for the reduction in productivity. There are a bunch of other reasons like late engineering, lack of information, procurement of equipment, availability of skilled labor, and late delivery of materials. Training a worker on how to use a harness doesn't delay a project. Delays in buying the harness and getting them to the site does.

- Treat people the way you would want to be treated. Have fun—and don't forget to laugh. You can be safe and productive and have a great day at work at the same time, but always stay focused. Treat each job you do as though it were a high-hazard job. Look at each job you do carefully and examine the steps and their sequences. You will feel better, feel more confident, and find more enjoyment. When you know what to do and how to do it, follow the rules of safe work and you will be safely productive.

Dean fears that when the economy slows down and the focus for many construction companies is primarily profit that the advancements in working toward being safely productive will be watered down. He hopes there are owners and developers who still maintain a sense of integrity when it comes to ensuring the safety of the workforce and that we don't go back in time. He acknowledges that residential and commercial construction never achieved the results that industrial projects achieved, and he attributes that to those sectors never fully embracing the safely productive movement. Commercial contractors will often not procure rebar or other services from companies that build safety into their work execution and delivery plans. They will often opt for the much cheaper solution putting safety-focused suppliers and subcontractors at a disadvantage in the marketplace.

We have ethically grown coffee, but we don't see any signs that say ethically built condos. This is mostly because new condo buyers probably don't care if the worker who built it wore a safety harness and was not allowed to smoke pot on breaks. As consumers and end users, we need to ask ourselves, "What value do we personally place on safe work?"

Here are some strategies that can help personality types like Dean stay engaged and working safely and productively:

- Get them involved in training. They will make the training fun, entertaining, and informative for participants. If they have challenges speaking in front of others, start them off with small groups while their confidence builds. If you stick with it, you will have a tremendous trainer who brings life to meetings, workshops, or conferences.
- Give them a project and let them take the lead. Give them a solid plan that encompasses safety and production and let them lead a small crew toward success. You will find that the challenger part of their personality is looking for opportunities to stand out and emerge as a leader. If you give them the opportunity and a solid plan, with their willingness to succeed, they will do just that.
- They have an inner drive to make the workplace better for all, and they'll look to do things innovatively to achieve that. They are often not stuck doing things one way and are open to looking at new and safer ways to improve productivity. If you have a challenge where the same old problems keep reoccurring, let them have a look. They can likely help with coming up with a safe and productive alternative.

Dean found the balance between being safe and productive within his three distinctive personality characteristics. He blends strong leadership instincts with a passion for making things better for everyone on the project—and he has a great time doing it.

I think I will see Dean on another site one day, and I'm very much looking forward to it. I have found a new, deeper appreciation for what makes Dean Dean. I like him very much.

CHAPTER 11
SARAH: THE EQUIPMENT OPERATOR

Enneagram Test Scoring

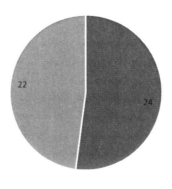

22

24

■ TYPE 4 INDIVIDUALIST   ■ TYPE 2 HELPER

I met Sarah, a twenty-six-year-old heavy equipment operator just after she was laid off and was looking for other work. I asked her about doing a personality test and interviewing her for this project. Initially, she seemed a little reluctant, but when I asked a few more questions, it became apparent that Sarah didn't think she would have anything to say that anyone would want to hear. I was so happy when she called back to say that she would participate and help in any way she could.

When I asked her about being safely productive, she said she really didn't have any insight into what leaders did, but she said she could speak for herself. Sarah was the youngest in a family of five children. She had wonderful parents and a good home life, but all throughout her childhood, she felt alone. She spent most of her time isolated with one or two friends, but she mostly spent time with her dog. Sarah was especially close to her oldest brother, who was almost twelve years older than she was. Her brother never seemed to have time for the other siblings, so the time he spent with her was all the more special.

Sarah graduated from a small-town high school and left to go to work in the city. She got a job working as a janitor in an industrial facility. She didn't think it was anything special, and she thought she wasn't very good at it. The other two women on her crew were older and seemed to have a much better work ethic. They were hard on Sarah, which made her feel isolated, unimportant, and alone.

Because of her oldest brother's good name, she got a call to go for an entry-level position with a trucking company. She happily accepted the position in an office environment. She was exposed to the many different elements of the transportation business, and she loved it. She formed close friendships at work and felt like part of a community. She was becoming a people person, and rather than isolating herself, she was happily engaged in life and enjoying many friends. She was in an awesome place and was offered a training role at a warehouse. She quickly made new friends and was earning a good wage.

She started to see, hear, and do more in safety. She became part of the emergency response team and actively engaged in their local union. The union sent her for occupational health and safety training, and she learned the rules around the work that she and her coworkers were engaged in. Up to that point, she hadn't thought too much about how safety fit into her job. She just tried to be careful and not get hurt.

As she received more information, training, and support, she became more engaged, and one day, she was elected to be the executive of the union. She worked closely with other members and found that many of the issues she was dealing with were related to safety—her colleagues were not following the rules, and were damaging heavy equipment and things like that—so she held biweekly union meetings. What was new was that the meetings would always start with safety. She would share information around legislation and incidents that happened on-site or elsewhere. She shared information on the collective agreement so people wouldn't find themselves in an infraction. She genuinely wanted the best for her team. The more she was involved and supported, the happier she was. They asked for more information, and the levels of engagement from the crew were on the rise.

On a night shift, she was in the warehouse when they got a call to respond to an emergency in the mine. Two heavy-hauler trucks had collided. An operator was pinned inside the cab by the steering column, but they were able to retrieve the worker without serious injury. The incident motivated Sarah to look at hazards around night-shift work, fatigue, and other incident causes. She was so engaged that she also began to look at the roadways in and out of the site. The highway was one of the worst in the region for collisions and fatalities. So, with her fellow union members, they lobbied the company to look at ways to improve conditions and safeguards coming to the site. Sarah was at her best, and she believed she was making the site safe, not just for herself, but for everyone who worked there.

By working safely, being known for a strong work ethic, and showing a desire to make things better, she was creating a culture of being safely productive. She did it without ever being aware it was happening. She was simply Sarah being the best Sarah she could be.

News came that the facility was closing down due to commodity prices. It was devastating to the communities that relied on the plant for employment and to the people who worked there. They had all been through so much as a team, and now they would all go their separate ways. Sarah was devastated.

When I talked to her, she was trying to remain optimistic during bad economic times. She felt like she had hit her stride, but now she felt like she was starting from square one. In a sea of resumes fighting for a few jobs, what would make her stand out? What would make her special? I believe this was the biggest challenge she would have to overcome. Here are some of her suggestions:

- Have pride, keep the equipment clean, and check it daily. When things are clean and orderly, you can't help but behave more professionally.
- Know what your equipment can and can't do. Read books, read online, and look at accidents that have happened with the equipment.
- Talk to more experienced operators about what they do to stop incidents before they happen. Find out how they stay productive and learn about more efficient ways to do your work. Treat them with the respect they are entitled to.
- Talk to the mechanics who take care of the equipment. If you can, stay while the work is being done and ask questions.
- Share what you know. Tell the people you work with, and they might start doing the same things.

Sarah is very wise, and I enjoyed her interview very much. She is incredibly in tune with others and looks both inside and outside of herself for answers.

To motivate someone with similar personality traits, supervisors should consider the following:

- Get them involved in a project or task that isn't routine. They can become bored and feel like they are not making a meaningful contribution if the work is the same every day.
- If possible, tasks should be focused on the fine finishing details that will make the site more appealing when clients and others come to see it.
- Let them know that the team is stronger because they are there. Talk to them, see them, and don't let them feel isolated or alone.

- Let them help others who are struggling. Bring them in to support or to look at a problem. They are highly innovative and can often see things that others may overlook.
- If they become moody or temperamental, something is wrong. Reengage them. When they are inspired, they will bring the best they have every day.

Her individualist personality was evident from the time she began to talk about her feelings of loneliness and how they uplifted her to feel unique. She has such incredible insights into other people and what they need as human beings. With the characteristics of her helper personality, she can't help but look around her and share her knowledge and insights in the hopes that it will help someone have a safer, more fulfilled day. It's ironic that she thought she wouldn't have anything worthwhile to say. Thank you, Sarah, for being you.

CHAPTER 12
NEXT STEPS

Who hasn't heard of a quality-control or quality-assurance program? It's a process of planning, doing, checking, and acting. We must ask ourselves if we want to live by chance or if we're going to live by design, and in that, lies a great opportunity. To live a life designed by you, your decisions, based on your highest values, personality strengths, and traits, is a life worth living.

After taking the Enneagram test, you will have a core understanding of who you can be when you're at your best. By taking this information and reading it—multiple times—you will gain a better sense of who you are and how you can create a plan to reach your best self.

Now, let's talk about the process for putting all we have learned together into action. Before each workweek starts, review your Enneagram results, formulate your plan, and decide how you will execute and assess its effectiveness. We will begin by looking at the four elements of the weekly cycle:

1. Identify your opportunity for growth and personal development this week.

2. Then, based on the opportunity you have selected, pick one or two things that you believe will bring you the most value in that area this week. Keep in mind how it could positively impact your needs, your safety performance, and your drive to be productive.

3. Have a weekly check-in and personal assessment. This is where we take a look at our level of development and report back to ourselves on the progress we made at work and off the job.

4. Work on forming new habits. What should you do more of? What should you do less of? What brought you the best results? How can you continue to experience growth and development?

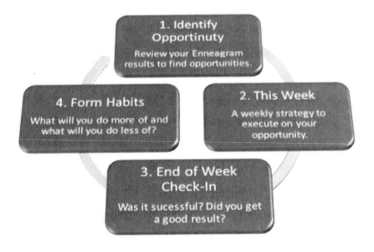

The Weekly Process Explained

By taking your Enneagram results and reviewing the qualities displayed when you are at your best, pick a single element to work on this week and create an action item around this for yourself this week. For example, let's take a look at a couple of personality types so I can illustrate what I'm talking about.

Example 1: Type 1 (The Reformer)

Identify the Opportunity

At their best, a reformer (type 1) is caring and compassionate and inspires others to be the same.

Weekly Action Item for the Reformer

With dignity and respect, check on a coworker who may be struggling and teach them something that helped you when you were learning a task. It could be a new worker who isn't quite sure where the tool room is or the correct doffing of a face shield. Involve others and ask what they do to prevent injury or make things more efficient. When putting tools away, you could also ensure they are safely stored and left in a way that you would want to find them.

End-of-Week Check-In

Do an assessment of yourself. How did it work? How did it feel? Did it help others? Did you see a change in others? Have a quick look to see where you are on your level of development scale.

Forming the Habit

Decide which of your strategies brought you the best results. What brings you up to the level of development and makes you feel whole? The more you practice this, the more it will become a habit.

Example 2: The Investigator (Type 5)

Identify The Opportunity

At their best, the investigator (type 5) is an intense visionary who is capable of extraordinary perception. They see the whole picture as well as details that many others may miss.

Weekly Action Item for the Investigator

Because you can become high-strung and intense, you need to schedule time for yourself to relax in healthy ways. Schedule some walks or a trip to the gym. Jogging can help you burn off excess energy and help you remain calm and focused. While at work, take the time to learn about a process, a tool, or piece of equipment. There are a multitude of resources you can draw from like product manuals, internet research, and drawings. Don't try to become an expert in everything. Select one small topic per week and do a deep dive looking for safety and productivity opportunities.

End-of-Week Check-In

Do an assessment of yourself. Do you feel good? Do you feel like some progress was made? Review your level of development scale. How safely productive was your mind-set?

Forming the Habit

When planning the next week, decide which of your strategies worked and which didn't. What brings you up the level of development? Practice and the habits will come.

Now It's Your Turn

Identify the Opportunity

Select something from your assessment, like the personal growth recommendations, your paradigms around the opportunity, or the top levels of the development scale. Pick one opportunity that you will work on this week.

To be at my best, I will focus on:

_____

_____

Weekly Action Items

Based on your selection, what will you do to improve your personal, safety, and productivity performance?

_____

_____

_____

End-of-Week Check-In

Do you feel good about your goal and how you executed it?

_____

_____

Did you have a safe and productive week? (Explain)

_____

_____

Where are you on your level of development? How are you feeling?

_____

_____

Forming The Habit

What can you do more of to support the development of a safely productive habit?

_____

_____

What should you do less of to rid yourself of unsafe and unproductive habits?

_____

_____

Tips for Weekly Planning

- Take a good look at your Enneagram results. Read through the sections and look at the things you would like to work on this week. Go easy and just pick one per week. Remember that lasting change doesn't happen overnight. It comes through a careful, methodical process of understanding what will bring you pride and gratification.
- Look through the personal growth recommendations for your personality type. This is a wonderful resource to help you stay on the right track and stay attuned to any changes—good or bad—that could be happening.
- When you select an opportunity, think about your paradigms around the opportunity and yourself. If you have doubts that you can achieve your goals and move up in the levels of development, challenge that paradigm. Remember that you have so much talent and the capacity to overcome challenges—and please don't sell yourself short.
- Assess how achieving your plan can positively impact safety and productivity. Safety means your security, well-being, and

productivity tap into your need for fulfillment and achievement; they are both equally important factors in the process.

- Find a quiet place to think about your plan, your strategies, and how success can ultimately help you. Make sure you do your planning before your workweek starts so you have it when your shift begins. Having a greater sense of purpose will help you execute the daily tasks in front of you.

- Try not to become discouraged if you don't see immediate results. Profound change takes time. The purpose of all of this is to help you get to a safely productive mind-set and make the work site better. You can achieve this through work and accountability to keep the commitments you make to yourself. Have faith and keep working the weekly process.

- Be kind to yourself. You deserve much kindness and support through all of this. There is so much information available through the Enneagram Institute, and many books and publications can help you delve into your personality traits. The more reading and research you do, the more gifts you will uncover. The biggest one is that you will truly know yourself and what you are capable of achieving.

I'm excited for you to try this process! Having a strategy to follow and time lines you can be accountable to isn't new. However, this time, you are in the driver's seat. You are making plans that will guide you toward being safely productive and using your greatest strengths and traits to help support yourself. This is truly about you, and the weekly plans will be meaningful only to you. It's not a one-size-fits-all plan. Each individual makes up a strong, safely productive team.

CHAPTER 13
SOLIDLY IN YOUR CORNER

What do I want to tell you before I leave you?

- Don't ever sell yourself short. I mean that from the bottom of my heart. Don't give up on yourself. Don't forget that there's no one like you. You are one of a kind, and there is a whole industry out there rooting for you, especially me.
- Don't be led by feelings only. They can be deceptive and do not always reflect reality.
- Know yourself. Read and learn about yourself through your Enneagram results. Keep watch on the levels of development. It is a valuable tool to help you self-monitor and keep yourself moving forward.
- Safety is about the choices you make. Make sure your decisions are based on sound information and not feelings or improvisation. You can do this.
- Lastly, remember that you may not be able to change an industry overnight, but you can focus on your own productivity and start there. We can have a safely productive culture where it's a win-win for all. If we change the culture, we change the game.

You are a unique combination of your paradigms, experiences, and personality traits. There is no one exactly like you, and I think you are an amazing gift to this industry. I want you to have all that's good in this life—to be happy, content, safe, and feeling good about what you've accomplished today. You have all of this ability within you. Take every opportunity to learn about yourself and find ways to stay performing at your highest level of development. That is where you will find fulfillment.

You don't have to rely on others to gain a sense of self-worth and happiness. You have the ability in you. I have faith that you can do anything that you decide you are going to do.

Be accountable. When it comes to zero harm, you have the best hand to play. Never harm yourself physically or by letting your inside voice tell you that you're not smart enough, good enough, or educated enough. That's just bullshit. I'm telling you this because I have said terrible things to myself: "Why are you so stupid! You look terrible in that! Go and change! You sound stupid." If I talked to my friends like that, I wouldn't have any—but why is it okay for us to be so mean to ourselves? It's just plain unacceptable. Never do it.

Your safety and your sense of pride and accomplishment are tied to your paradigms about yourself. Do you remember when I asked you to write down the first word that came to your mind about engineers? Well, what is the first word that pops into your head when you think of yourself?

If it's a good, healthy, uplifting-your-soul kind of word, then great! I'm in full agreement. If it's negative, demeaning, or makes you feel bad, it's time to look within. Look deep and find out why. What are your paradigms about yourself? Answer honestly.

I know it's hard—and it's sometimes unbearable—but get to know yourself and research the levels of development. Keep a close watch on where you are. If you're sliding, talk to someone you trust. You will see that you're not alone, and that's the most important first step. And for heaven's sake, be that ear for someone else who might be trouble. When you understand the personality types, you will see when people close to you are suffering. Even if you just have a vague sense that someone you care about is not quite themselves, please just ask if they are okay and if they need to talk about anything.

Change is inevitable. We spend most of our lives working and trying to learn how to get through all of this. By the time we think we have it figured out, some unexpected life event comes crashing through the door.

When change happens, see it for what it really is. Be logical, thoughtful, and smart about it. Changes can have an impact on you far more than you may realize. If you try to push them down and pretend they don't matter, you are likely sending yourself down a couple notches on your level of development. When you start to slide, everything is impacted, including your focus on safety and being productive.

When you have been down or been thinking of giving up, have you ever jumped out of bed determined to bring your best to working safely and productively?

You need to put yourself first before taking care of others. By doing this, you will be better at everything else. There is nothing more important than you, your heart, your soul, and your safety. Use your strengths and learn from your challenges.

I want nothing more than for you to be safe, happy, content, and fulfilled at work and in life. I will always be solidly in your corner.

THE ERIKA LEGACY FOUNDATION

If you or someone you know is in a crisis, one of the best resources to help construction folks is the Erika Legacy Foundation.

Erika was an adventurer, an educator, and a warrior. She was kind and compassionate, and she wanted to make the world a better place. Erika was a visionary who believed people had greatness within them, and she knew success was something we could all achieve. Erika was a construction worker.

The Erika Legacy Foundation was set up to continue her work and spread her passion for helping others become the best they could be: to be happy, secure, safe, and excelling in all areas of their life. Her foundation helps construction workers get help by bringing awareness and dialogue to mental wellness issues that the people of construction and their families face.

Visit the website at www.erikalegacy.com. Help where you can, give where you can, and spread the word to your site about this tremendous person and the foundation that humbly shares her name.

A percentage of sales proceeds from *Safely Productive* goes to support the Erika Legacy Foundation so they can continue their work in providing mental health and wellness programs for all.